WHO'S LEADING —YOUR— BUSINESS?

Conquer the "Monstrous" Challenges of Vision, Values, Processes and More

LIZ PARKER

Nicholas J. Tucker, Jr. Illustrator

Who's Leading Your Business? Conquer the "Monstrous" Challenges of Vision, Values, Processes and More © Copyright 11.20.2022

Elizabeth R. (Liz) Parker, Nicholas J. Tucker, Jr. Illustrator, Greer, SC

For more information, email Liz@LTResults.com

ISBN: (paperback) 979-8-88759-336-4

ISBN: (ebook) 979-8-88759-337-1

ISBN: (hardcover) 979-8-88759-373-9

Get Your Free Gift!

To get the best experience with this book, I've found readers who download and use

High Performance Checklist — 9 Solutions to Conquer the "Monstrous" Challenges in Your Business
are able to implement faster and take the next steps needed to create the organization you envisioned.

You can get a copy by visiting:

www.LTResults.com/monsterbook/resources

High Performance Checklist
9 SOLUTIONS TO CONQUER THE "MONSTROUS" CHALLENGES IN YOUR BUSINESS

What's the status of yours?

Monster Chapter	Solution Factor	Danger	Caution	Working	Am I Dr. Jekyll	Am I Mr. Hyde	Both at times?
	Shared Mission & Vision	○	○	○	☐	☐	☐
	Organizational Chart — Roles & Responsibilities	○	○	○	☐	☐	☐
	Link to Values — Beliefs turn into Actions	○	○	○	☐	☐	☐
	Understand & Engage — Know Others' Needs	○	○	○	☐	☐	☐
	Top Chaos Creators — Processes to Restore Calm	○	○	○	☐	☐	☐
	In Control of Stress & Emotions	○	○	○	☐	☐	☐
	On Top of Cashflow — Give to Others	○	○	○	☐	☐	☐
	No More Turmoil — Leadership & Culture	○	○	○	☐	☐	☐
	Stay the Course! — Use Action Plans	○	○	○	☐	☐	☐
THIS MONTH:	Our Focus is:	○	○	○	☐	☐	☐

LT Results and Mouth-agape.com

® 2022 Who's Leading Your Business? Conquer the "Monstrous" Challenges of Vision, Values, Processes and More

Dedication

To the Leaders who read this book. This is a quest; it will take time and patience. With focus, clear beliefs and values your leadership will evolve and you will create the organization you envision. Please know other leaders are experiencing similar situations. You are never alone. Reach out.

To my clients, who have also become my friends — when we follow the giving principle in our lives, we each feel richer in our relationships and more fulfilled with what we bring to this world.

This book is for you.

Table of Contents

INTRODUCTION

Could there be Monsters in your business?

Does your business ever experience high employee turnover, missed deadlines, poor accountability, cost overruns, or failed projects? Do you wonder if you could have blind spots regarding your business–things you don't even know are issues?

Have you ever felt so overwhelmed by your business that you don't know where to start? Or had moments when you wondered, "Could I be the problem?"

If you answered "Yes" to any of the above, or if you feel your business is off track and not achieving its goals, I invite you to take a trip with me, a quest to identify:

"What are the blind spots in my business?"

"What behaviors are undermining my business?"

Just as blind spots can generate problems, so can poorly handled behaviors. Recall the story of Dr. Jekyll and Mr. Hyde. Dr. Jekyll portrayed the best aspects of the character; Mr. Hyde was his dark side. In this book we will compare your leadership behaviors to those of Dr. Jekyll and Mr. Hyde. When our behavior is like the professional Dr. Jekyll, things run well. We involve the team, set expectations, delegate to employees, and accomplish goals. Conversely, there may be moments that we act like the reactionary Mr. Hyde. We are inconsistent, indecisive, and eruptive with our teams or customers, creating business havoc and spawning hidden monsters in our wake.

If you join me on this quest, you will hunt down and slay monstrous problems that lie hidden in the shadows of your business. There will be no pitchforks or wooden stakes, but with some diligence and introspection on your part, you will be armed with resources as effective as silver bullets in overcoming hidden monstrous challenges.

You will:

- Learn nine business solutions that every high performing organization utilizes.
- Identify blind spots and root causes that feed your business issues.
- Apply appropriate solutions to address challenges quickly and effectively.
- Reflect on how problems are managed and determine if you and your leadership team have handled them from a professional Dr. Jekyll approach or reactionary Mr. Hyde perspective.

In the end, you'll have a clear picture of what monsters bedevil your business, how to be rid of them for good and how you can be a peak performing leader.

I have learned what I'm sharing through 40 years of business experience and 23 years of owning a strategic consulting business, LT Results. I have garnered the information and successes in this book from my years of working with all types of businesses, from small family-run enterprises to multi-national corporations.

When I started my business in Hong Kong in 1999, I worked in a unique consortium with several competitors to achieve a common goal for our non-profit clients. Prior to that experience, I viewed other consultants as competitors. However, when we consultants all worked together, we created more opportunities for everyone and best practices came through quickly. Sharing ideas provided the best possible solutions for our clients. I learned then that abundant thinking creates unlimited possibilities, and I incorporate it into all my coaching.

I returned to the U.S. in 2001 and 2010 I made my home in Greenville, SC. I worked with family businesses, locally and nationally. It dawned on me that these small and medium-sized family businesses had organizational issues similar to the larger, multinational, non-family corporations I had worked with internationally.

I noticed that in both of these types of organizations destructive interpersonal dynamics and leadership disconnects occur and cause blind spots in the business. We each come to work with our own baggage and hang-ups from childhood, adult, and home environments; at times that baggage emerges to play out in the workplace.

Some people can compartmentalize their baggage and keep it separate from the workplace, while others cannot. When they cannot, the behaviors will show up in the company's interpersonal dynamics. When these dynamics present in owners or leaders, they have a significant impact on the entire business and its performance.

If you own or lead a business you need to avoid these types of pitfalls to ensure success. Your time is valuable, so this book offers quick and practical ways to do that. In a short time, you will:

- Learn to quickly correct existing issues.
- Identify problems you can avoid by acting proactively.
- Gain focus, insight, and tools to get the results you want and need–faster and more cost effectively.
- Have some fun along the way!

WARNING:

Be aware that if you read this book, see your own situation, then decide to ignore or wait to implement the relevant points—**you are in dangerous territory.** Every moment you choose not to make a decision about a problem or issue in your business, someone else in your company will take control and decide for you.

When this happens, you are consciously (or subconsciously) choosing to have diminished effectiveness, unhappy employees, less personal time, and less money. Do not wait. I urge you to read this book and apply the solutions suggested. The results will positively impact you, your business, and the people around you.

This is serious information, but don't fret–we're also going to have fun, especially with the illustrations. Nicholas (Cole) Tucker, Jr., is this book's illustrator. A graduate of the School of Visual Arts in Manhattan, N.Y., his signature in the art world is mouth-agape.com. One of Cole's talents is creating character-filled monsters. He has brought my business monsters to life with humor and wit to highlight points made throughout the book.

So, if you're up for this quest, turn the page. Your company's first monster may show up as destructive behavior within your life.

CHAPTER 1

You and Your Business—Who's Leading?

Welcome Leader. Your story starts now! We have a new way of working post-pandemic. Some work virtually, while others are back on-site. Business expectations have changed, and we continue to see situations we never anticipated before.

The setting for this story is *your* company. Some of you work in offices, some are on plant sites, some work remotely, and some lead from multiple locations and offices. This story is based in *your* location, wherever that is. If you are there, the story is there.

You are my main character. Whether you call yourself an entrepreneur, a business owner, or leader, we are going on a journey, a quest together. Every good trip has a reason to begin, and in our case, that reason is a conflict between your business passion and your personal relationships.

Business Passion vs. Personal Relationships

At times we may need to spend more time in our business, and our personal relationships take a back seat. That is a continuing struggle for a business leader. It is not usually a problem unless business time repeatedly overrides personal time, and you break commitments.

Have you experienced a situation like one of these?

- Your spouse or partner is at the end of their rope. They have had enough!

- You are never home, the kids never see you, and you routinely miss family dinner and bedtime.

- Your family can rarely plan trips because there's not enough money in the business at that time to travel.

- Every time your family tries to do fun activities, you have a business emergency to resolve.

- You planned a trip. But your spouse and kids go on ahead, and you stay behind to put out the fire.

- You do get away, but not for long because the business cannot operate without you.

- Your spouse has said, more than once, that you are missing out on your kids' lives.

Dear Leader, this story is about you and for you, especially if any of the above situations fit. Let's dig a little deeper. Have you heard any of these from your spouse or family members?

- "It's like you are two people: One moment nice as pie, the second, a monster! You're either withdrawn and silent, or you are angry and shouting at us!" (See Chapter 6)

- "You don't keep your promises. You say you'll be here, but you aren't. So even if we don't go anywhere, you aren't home with us." (See Chapter 3)

- "When you are here, you are not mentally here. You're on your phone, computer, or tablet at all hours of the day and night, not even putting it down on weekends." (See Chapter 5).

- "You can't seem to make a decision and stick to it. One moment you decide, and then you take it back the next." (See Chapter 5)

- "Why did you even start this business?" (See Chapter 2)

- "Where's the money? We're always waiting for the next check." (See Chapter 7)

- "Do you even think about me or the children when you make your plans? Let me remind you when we were on lockdown, you acted like nothing was wrong and left us to go to work! I was scared to death to even go pick up groceries! The kids couldn't go to school. Someone had to stay home with our children and teach them! Guess who had to do that? ME, my career had to go on hold. Not yours." (See Chapter 4)

- "You hire all these people, and then you don't even let them run the company. You have to be involved in everything!" (See Chapters 2 & 5)

- "You mumble that your employees can't be trusted or can't learn what to do. Well, whose fault is that?" (See Chapters 4 & 5)

- "The piece that infuriates me the most is when that large order came in. Your two key employees just plain quit. You made all of us go in and work to get that order out.

We had to stop our plans to do your employees' work!" (See Chapter 8)

- "What is going on with you?" (The book)

If you've heard any of these, then you need to pay close attention to this book. They are warning signs that should make you stop in your tracks and recognize the problems going on around you, with your business approach and your relationships. In my experience, it's most likely that the issues your family has with your business also indicate that key areas within your business are out of alignment. You might have monsters lurking in your organization.

Don't despair. Each chapter of this book will address topics that could be the root of your problems and source of your monsters. You may have more than one problem. Or one problem could be a symptom of others. (Monsters love company!)

For example, let's say your family complains there is never enough money. You think, "Hey, it's just a cash flow issue." But the problem keeps occurring, the family keeps complaining, and you finally decide to resolve it. (Chapter 7) As you investigate, you notice that the poor cash flow occurs because checks aren't being processed as they arrive. (Chapter 4) You are the only one who manages cash flow, and you've been too busy to stay on top of it. You realize that as your business has grown, you have not defined or refined roles for your team to handle deposits. (Chapter 2) What initially appeared as a cash flow issue was not the core problem. The root of the problem was undefined organizational roles and responsibilities.

Once you define these roles, you can create clear processes for handling payments to ensure ample cash flow. So you see, when you address the root cause of your problem, you can solve it, remove the monster, and restore harmony.

The next question is, how does your organization manage problems? How do you respond when things do not go smoothly? Does someone lose their temper and act like "a monster rearing its ugly head"? With problems also come behaviors to address them. We've all been in situations where we behaved less than ideally, and in those situations, our language and actions could have been considered downright rude and inappropriate.

As we work together to resolve your organizational problems, you need to observe your and your team's behaviors. Are individuals (or you) acting like *monsters* to others in certain situations? In other words, do you act unprofessionally or rude when dealing with others? Try to understand which situations bring the monsters out. Then you can figure out how to eliminate those monsters so your business can operate more efficiently.

To add a little fun, when discussing behaviors throughout the book, I will ask you to determine if you (or others) appear to be acting like Dr. Jekyll or the menacing Mr. Hyde. Robert Louis Stevenson's 1886 novella *The Strange Case of Dr. Jekyll and Mr. Hyde* is a classic example of the two sides of an individual's behavior, good and evil.

Dr. Henry Jekyll

Stevenson describes Dr. Henry Jekyll as "a large, well-made, smooth-faced man of 50, with something of a stylish cast perhaps, but every mark of capacity and kindness."

Jekyll is a member of the English Victorian upper class. He attends dinner parties and has drinks with elite professionals. But behind that façade, he struggles to maintain social decorum. He wants to fulfill his darker desires but knows he cannot. So, he develops a serum that changes him into a different person, so he can experience new things anonymously.

Mr. Edward Hyde

Mr. Edward Hyde is the creature that Jekyll turns into after taking the serum. While Jekyll takes part in the upper-class activities, Hyde lives in darkness. He is brutish and violent.

In addition, Hyde is described as short, stocky, and "ape-like." The author, writing in the late 1800s, was suggesting that he is a degenerate, proof that the human species is descending rather than progressing. Stevenson specifically describes him as "pale and dwarfish, he gave an impression of deformity without any nameable malformation."

Please consider the following as you read this book:

- ☐ As an owner or leader, you have strengths. Are those expressed by your Dr. Jekyll traits?

- ☐ If you don't deal well with certain business topics or issues (i.e., don't lead, don't manage your team, or the opposite and act silent and withdrawn) consider those actions as Mr. Hyde traits, as they are menacing.

- ☐ Merriam-Webster's dictionary defines menace as: "one that represents a threat: DANGER, or annoying person."

☐ Your role in this book is to discern when you (or others) behave as Dr. Jekyll or Mr. Hyde.

☐ Let's assume that we all inherently want to be Dr. Jekyll and display appropriate responses and leadership in every situation.

☐ There may be times you're uncertain if you behave like Dr. Jekyll or Mr. Hyde. It will require self-reflection. If you continue to be stuck, ask for input from a trusted co-worker or family member who sees you in your work setting.

☐ Realize that hearing feedback about yourself can be extremely difficult. Prepare yourself to listen and not react.

At the end of each chapter, you will review its topic and then replay in your mind how you and others behave in those situations—like Dr. Jekyll or Mr. Hyde—and then take action steps to choose the behavior you truly want to exhibit.

Let's try it out. Consider the use of sarcasm in business communication.

Merriam-Webster's dictionary defines **Sarcasm** as: "the use of irony to mock or convey contempt." In other words, it can be using words that mean the opposite of what the speaker intends, especially to insult or show irritation with someone, or to amuse others.

I hear sarcasm and other types of humor used in office communication regularly. Sarcasm can be viewed as humor, but often, it is seen as cruelly making fun of a situation or an individual.

Some people use sarcasm to share their true feelings in a mocking way, rather than being direct and having a one-on-one conversation about important topics.

I once worked with an owner who used sarcasm extensively with his sales force. He would say things like, "Oh, you decided to call on a customer today?" Or "You actually sold something?" He made sarcastic comments rather than referencing the salesperson's calendar or having a regularly scheduled one-on-one conversation about their call schedule or performance. Sarcasm can damage relationships if it is the only way you communicate.

 **Moment to Change**

Ask yourself, "Am I Dr. Jekyll or Mr. Hyde by using sarcasm as humor within my communication style?"

Am I Dr. Jekyll?	Am I Mr. Hyde?
You use sarcasm in your communication style to be fun and lighten a moment in a friendly manner. *Be sure no one is being ridiculed or insulted.*	You use sarcasm in your communication style to poke fun and ridicule with insult, intentionally hurting or shaming an individual. Not speaking directly.

Regardless of which personality you are, we can improve. Please answer the following:

1. What must I stop doing because it doesn't work?
2. What could I start doing to make it better or more appropriate?
3. What could I continue doing that I'm doing well?

Now that you see how the book is designed and have had some practice, let's jump right in. Do you remember why you started your business?

CHAPTER 2

Remember Why You Started this Business –Set a Shared Mission and Vision for Organizational Clarity

Spouse & Family's comment,

"Why did you even start this business?"

Dear Leader, did you start your business dreaming of being your own boss? Did you have a grand vision of what you wanted to accomplish? Or were you like me, and just kind of fell into your business?

I never dreamed of having my own business initially, but today I would fight tooth and nail for it. I have realized the freedom to be and do what I enjoy with people I like, when I like. Owning a well-run business can be hugely satisfying but leading a floundering business can be draining. Let me help you stay on track for success.

The key to keeping a business purposeful and rewarding is organizational clarity. In this chapter, I will share the importance of having a clear purpose, and then show you how to use that as a guiding light. I will show you how to build measurable goals around your vision to make it a reality.

You will also examine the importance of clearly delineating organizational roles and responsibilities. By following my recommendations, you will possess the tools to "right the ship" should your business ever go off course.

If your business has no stated purpose or vision, it's never too late to start. As you may recall from the introduction, I unexpectedly went from employee to business owner over a weekend—in a foreign country. Even though I'd been living in Hong Kong and was familiar with it, I had already packed to return to the U.S. as I was jobless.

Do you think I had planned my vision and knew what my company was going to do? Heck no! I had to do the work I had been contracted to do and find a new place to live as I'd already moved out of my apartment and thought I was finished in Hong Kong. Over the course of my first year as an entrepreneur, I found the energy and time to develop a strategic plan for my business. Since then, I continue to tweak—and sculpt—my plan to stay current with my clients' needs. You, too, will want to continue to revise and update your plan to keep your company relevant to your market.

Throughout my consulting career, I've designed tools to streamline the process of uncovering purpose and vision. I'll share those with you to make the process as fast and efficient as possible. So, let's start! How far are you in realizing the dreams you had for your company? Does it look the way you had hoped?

How do you feel about where your business is today? Really think about this answer.

A. Happy

B. Not happy or sad

C. Sad about where the business is today

D. Disappointed about where you are at this point in your business journey

If you're happy, congratulations! I might assume you are like Dr. Jekyll and carefully planned your business. If it isn't quite the dream you had in mind, did some changes occur along the way, such as:

- Family conflicts happened?

- Partner conflicts, people left or people changed?

- Market changed?

- Opportunity for different products or services occurred?

- Idea went away?

- Were too slow to market?

- Lacked funding? No other money to use?

- Took more resources than planned?

- Financial backing withdrew or left?

- Lost desire?

- Got bored and didn't follow through?

- Were afraid, anxious about taking the risk?

- Didn't persist?

- Became overwhelmed?

- Lost it in divorce?

- Something else happened?

I am sorry if any of these happened to you. Life can knock you upside the head when you least expect it. When that happens, you must ask yourself and decide, "How badly do I want this business to continue?"

Starting and running your own business means you must take a stand from time to time. It takes courage to face difficult challenges. If you have doubts, who will help you out? You must dig deep down and find your passion, the inner voice that gives you guidance and direction. Resilience and persistence are two key traits necessary for entrepreneurs. You will call on these traits to sustain your business.

"When something is important enough, you do it even if the odds are not in your favor."
—Elon Musk

Do *you* want to change the business from where it is today? Your answer is important. If it's a yes, you need to believe it's a yes, because:

"Doubt kills more dreams than failure ever will."
—Susy Kassem

I'm going to assume you confidently said "YES": You want to change your business from where it is today. If it isn't working the way you desire, it probably lacks clarity and direction. You will have to do some things differently to improve results. Let's get to work.

To start, ask yourself, do you have a mission, vision, or some other goal statement written down today?

Circle one: **Yes**   **No**

Great. That gets us going. If you did not circle an answer, was it because:

1. You had one but didn't update it.

2. You had one but didn't list goals.

3. You had one but it sat on your shelf and collected dust—no one looked at it or executed it.

4. You didn't know you should have one.

Recent research supports your urgent need for a vision.

> *Studies have shown a full 20% of small businesses fail in their first year, 30% in their second year, and 50% by year five. A full 70% of small businesses don't make it past their tenth birthday.... Here are eight common reasons small businesses fail.*
>
> *No vision*
>
> *No niche*
>
> *No business plan*
>
> *No marketing plan*
>
> *No action*
>
> *No commitment to learning*
>
> *No follow-up, 8) No consistency.*
>
> *(Laura Cowan, "Eight Common Reasons Small Businesses Fail," Forbes, Oct. 24, 2019).*

The solution is to have a mission and vision. Some people use these terms interchangeably, while others have more specific definitions. You can call these concepts whatever you like as long as **you** know what they are. It's your business.

This is how I define them. **Mission** is your reason for starting the business. It answers the question, why you exist? It shares with others how you will be impacting the world with this business.

Here are some examples:

1. **LinkedIn:** "Connect the world's professionals to make them more productive and successful."

2. **Tesla:** "To accelerate the advent of sustainable transport by bringing compelling mass-market electric cars to market as soon as possible."

3. **Shopify:** "To make commerce better for everyone."

Vision is a short statement that encompasses **the ideal future state** the company would like to realize based on its mission. It is a road map. It inspires and leads to the future. A strong company vision makes employees want to serve a company to achieve its vision. A vision may seem impossible to achieve or even imagine how to accomplish. Examples are:

1. **LinkedIn:** "Create economic opportunity for every member of the global workforce."

2. **Tesla:** "Create the most compelling car company of the 21st century by driving the world's transition to electric vehicles."

3. **Shopify:** "Make commerce better for everyone, so businesses can focus on what they do best: building and selling their products."

Let's dig into this further to help you identify your company's mission and vision.

Mission (The Why):

The decision-making authority for your business should answer the following questions. If you are the owner, that is you. If you are a leader, but not the owner, reading this book, you can guide the owners on what to do next.

Mission—some refer to it as vision—inspires a business to something beyond itself, besides making money. These additional questions help clarify why you exist. "What world problems do you solve? What causes do you champion? What do you strive to do to improve in the world?"

I've seen owners get stuck right here and believe they are in it only to make money, but please don't stop there. Consider why making money is important. What will it do for others?

A method to dig deep and ensure you've gotten to your true reason is to ask yourself, 'why your mission exists' five times in a row. This is a lean management principle that works well here. You are trying to get to the larger aspirational reason for why your business exists. This core reason will emotionally attract and connect customers, employees, investors, etc. to your company. Your mission statement becomes a magnet drawing like-minded people to your dream. To help you further understand the power of this principle I recommend you watch Simon Sinek's TED Talk, Start with Why on YouTube at: https://www.youtube.com/watch?v=u4ZoJKF_VuA to further understand the impact your company's mission has on others.

Now let's get to work on documenting your mission. For this next exercise, get outside and connect to nature. Answers may come more easily. Clear your mind. Become quiet and reflective. This will help you hear your inner dialogue, your intuition, the still small voice that guides you. Write down the first things that come to mind as you read the question. Don't judge, just answer, and go on to the next question.

MISSION EXERCISE ONE - YOUR COMPANY:

1. What is the mission of your business?

2. Why does it exist?

3. Why is that important?

4. Why is that important?

5. Why is that important?

6. And why is that important?

This final answer, #6 will be what your true reason for existing is.

Our Mission is: _____

MISSION EXERCISE ONE - EXAMPLE:

1. What is the mission of your business? **To make money.**

2. Why does it exist? **To sell electric cars.**

3. Why is that important? **It provides a more cost-effective and environmentally safe way to transport people.**

4. Why is that important? **It is less harmful to our planet.**

5. Why is that important? **People will live longer because resources still exist.**

6. Why is that important? **It provides stability to our planet while allowing people to move freely around.**

There it is, #6's answer. That's the real reason, this is the car example's Mission! **It provides stability to our planet while allowing people to move freely around.**

Still feeling stuck? Consider this:

"You don't have to be great to start, but you have to start to be great." —Zig Ziglar

Let those words sink into your soul. I love this quote because it takes the pressure off. Remember, you don't have to do this perfectly. Even a poor start will get you to a great finish eventually, but YOU HAVE TO START.

It often takes more than one attempt, so here is a second method to get to your why. I encourage you to do both types of exercises to discover if your answer comes out the same. If you end up with two different answers consider combining them to create one more aspirational and emotionally engaging "why" mission statement.

MISSION EXERCISE TWO EXAMPLE: The same electric car dealership used the second method.

1. What do we do: **We sell electric cars.**
2. What's the benefit of that? **We help people drive in an environmentally friendly way.**
3. What's the benefit of that? **It reduces pollution caused by driving.**
4. What's the benefit of that? **It reduces human-contribution to climate change.**
5. What's the benefit of that? **It reduces harm to life on Earth.**

Mission Exercise Two Car Example is: **<u>Provide a life-sustaining method of travel.</u>**

Now, it's your turn to use your company information here:

MISSION EXERCISE TWO - YOUR COMPANY:

1. **What do we do:**
2. **What's the benefit of that?**
3. **What's the benefit of that?**
4. **What's the benefit of that?**
5. **What's the benefit of that?**

The Mission is: _____

Final Step

From our example, take the answers from both exercises. Look at them and decide if one is better than the other or if you should consolidate them.

Answer from Mission Exercise 1: **It provides stability to our planet while allowing people to move freely around.**

Answer from Mission Exercise 2: Provide a life-sustaining method of travel.

Our example company's innovative mission is:

> **To accelerate the advent of sustainable transport by bringing compelling mass-market electric cars to market as soon as possible.** – Tesla

YOUR TURN FOR YOUR COMPANY:

Take the answers from both exercises. Look at them and decide if one is better than the other or if they should be consolidated.

Answer from Mission Exercise 1:_____

_____

Answer from Mission Exercise 2: _____

_____

Your Company Mission is:

Congratulations!! Discovering your company's mission will transform your day-to-day operations. You will bring meaning into the workplace and connect with the emotions of your employees and customers just by sharing your "why."

VISION (The Road map):

Next is your vision statement. How does your "why" affect your business? It is important to turn your why into a vision, which is a short statement that serves as a strategic road map for your company.

Remember, **Vision** is what you want your company to **idealistically** accomplish. It is a direction. It inspires and leads your employees and customers into the future reality.

"Good business leaders create a vision, articulate the vision, passionately act on the vision, and relentlessly drive it to completion."—Jack Welch

To create a vision, owners and executives define what they want the company to strive to accomplish as it relates to their mission. The vision will seem impossible to achieve or even hard to imagine how it will ever be accomplished. The point is to set the direction. You don't need to know "how" you'll accomplish it today. That will come as time passes and your business evolves.

A vision statement contains certain elements. It should be:

- Challenging: Not too easy to achieve.
- Clear: One objective.
- Concise: Simple, easy to read, and can be memorized.
- Future-Oriented: What the company strives to be long-term.
- Inspiring: Will excite those involved.
- Unique: Unlike anything else.

- Time-Definite: A fixed point in the future to achieve and evaluate your vision statement.

Let's start with an exercise to get your creative juices flowing. I call it, "What's the Headline?"

Think ahead to 20 years from today. What year will it be? How will you read news and see headlines? Imagine that medium and think about your business then. What ground-breaking headline would you like to see about your business?

Here is one I'd like to see in 2043: **"LT Results reaches vision! Impacts owners and leaders worldwide to create high performing organizations by unlocking hidden potential."**

Now, you try it. Keep in mind your company's mission and values (if you know them). Write your draft vision statements (or headlines) below.

What challenging, future-oriented, inspiring, unique objective would you like to achieve 20 years from now?

-
-
-
-
-
-

Inspirational Visions to Reference:

- **Tesla:** "To create the most compelling car company of the 21st century by driving the world's transition to electric vehicles."

- **Starbucks:** "To inspire and nurture the human spirit—one person, one cup, and one neighborhood at a time."

- **Amazon:** "To be earth's most customer-centric company, where customers can find and discover anything they might want to buy online."

- **Feeding America:** "An America where no one is hungry."

- **Shopify:** "Make commerce better for everyone, so businesses can focus on what they do best: building and selling their products."

Reflect on your headline, if working with a group, discuss what you've written. Which headline aligns with your mission for why you exist and draws others to your business? What feels right to you? What makes you feel proud to say you're working to accomplish "x"?

Your Vision Statement is:

Bravo! Another piece complete (or at least started). If you're not quite there, that's okay. Let it sit in your subconscious, and it will reveal itself with time.

How do I know this works? Numerous client experiences. In one case, I worked with a 40+ year old family-owned-business that had

13 years with the same revenues and profitability. They couldn't seem to break through that level. They had done all the right things up to that point, but something wasn't moving the needle.

We discovered that the owners had never documented their mission, vision, and values. Once they realized they had never formally communicated this information through their network of offices and staff, they immediately went to work. They wrote down why they existed, what they were trying to accomplish with their vision, and how they were going to accomplish it. Voilà, the money gates opened!

THE DETAILS: (What, How, When, and Who)

Earlier in the chapter I mentioned the terms mission and vision are used interchangeably by the public. This is another one of the areas where this happens. Some define the term mission as the specific steps to take to accomplish the vision, not the definition of why you exist. This is your company, use the terms as they work for you. But make sure you define the terms for your employees and have the concepts written. This section of detail is incredibly important, so please don't skip this step.

You need to describe what your company does, how it does it, when specific actions will take place, and who will be involved to make it happen. Here are two different exercises to help you detail what you need to do to carry out your vision. Do one or both.

EXERICSE 1 – Write the Story

Go back to the headline exercise. Think about the headline you wrote that became your vision statement. Now add the details in the form of a news story. Explain how that vision was accomplished. Tell us who did what and how.

-
-
-
-
-
-
-

EXERCISE 2 - Six Clarifying Questions

"Six Clarifying Questions" is my favorite tool for putting your Who, What, When, and How together. These questions will form the basic structure for the business information you are about to assemble. For more, please read Patrick Lencioni, *The Advantage: Why Organizational Health Trumps Everything Else in Business*: Jossey-Bass, 2012, and *Silos, Politics, and Turf Wars*: Jossey-Bass, 2008.

The Six Clarifying Questions are:

1. Why do we exist? *(From your Mission - Why statement)*

2. How do we behave? *(Define in Chapter 3 and document on* Organizational Overview *form*, Fig. 2-1*)*

3. What do we do? *(Document on* Organizational Overview *form*, Fig. 2-1*)*

4. How will we succeed? (*Document on* Organizational Overview *form*, Fig. 2-1 & *podcast explanation)*

5. What is most important, right now? *(Document on* The Way Forward *form*, Fig. 2-2 *and through team conversations)*

6.   Who must do what? *(Document on* The Way Forward *Form,* Fig. 2-2)

These questions are simple and direct. By answering them, owners and leaders get to the core of their business and can lead with clarity and certainty.

Use the following two forms (*Organizational Overview,* Fig. 2-1, and *The Way Forward,* Fig. 2-2) to easily capture the answers to exercise 1 or 2 and complete your business's strategic plan.

By the end of Chapter 3, you and your team will be able to answer all six of the clarifying questions.

FILL IN THE ORGANIZATIONAL OVERVIEW FORM, Refer to Fig. 2-1

Why we Exist–That is your Why Statement (Mission) and answer to Question #1 from the Six Clarifying Questions.

Vision– From your headline exercise

10 Year Goal, and 3-5 Year Goals—Push yourself to think big and take a risk. You do not have to know how you will accomplish everything before you write it down. The answers and solutions will come. Be as specific and detailed as you can, knowing you will adjust these down the road.

What we value and how we behave—In Chapter 3, you will work to define your values. Once done, you will come back and add them here. This is also the answer to Question #2. However, you may have answers immediately come to mind. If so, write them in and review them when you finish Chapter 3.

What we do as our core business—Tell us your business, answer to Question #3.

Fig. 2-1 Organizational Overview.

To download go to: www.LTResults.com/monsterbook/resources

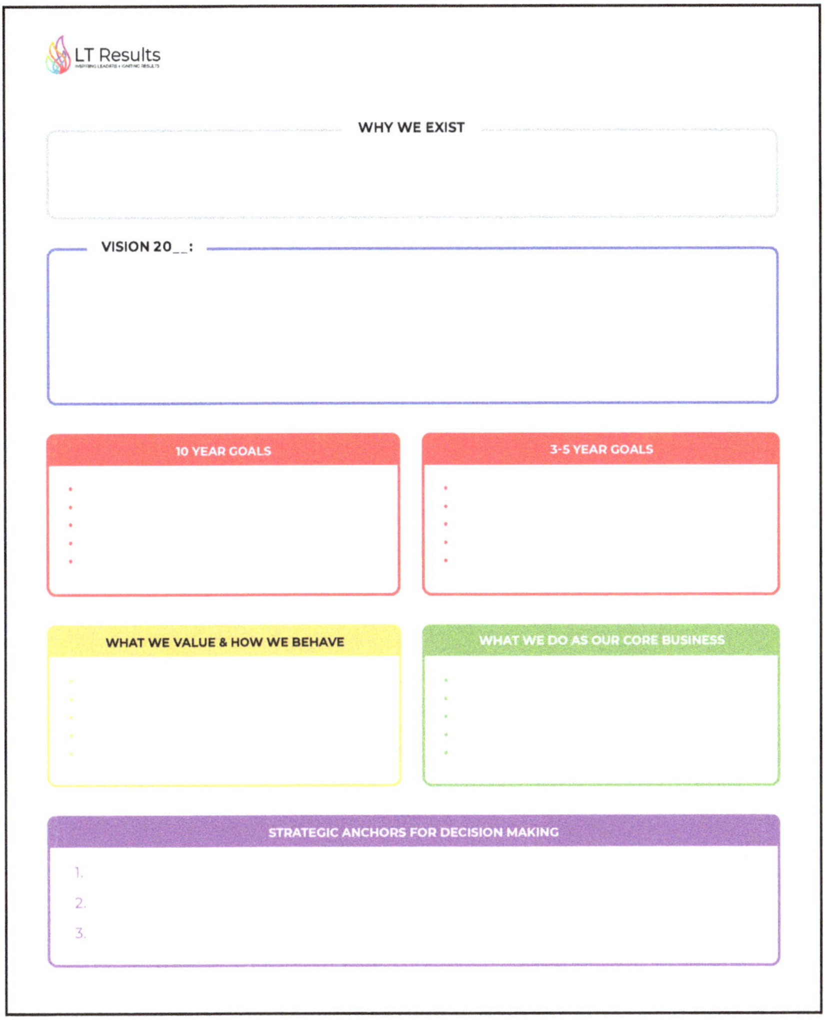

Strategic Anchors for Decision-Making

Strategic Anchors will act as a sort of litmus test for your business. The intent is to design three questions that will act as filters to drive all company decisions to align or serve the vision. A few examples of anchors are product superiority, lowest price in the market, and individualized service. They could refer to your three uniques of your secret sauce. Your Strategic Anchors will be specific to your business. I've had clients who struggled with this step and instead used questions like the following with success: "Will this decision help us reach our vision? Is the decision in line with our values? Does this decision yield x% return on investment in three years?" For a fuller understanding of this Patrick Lencioni concept, this podcast will help you identify your three strategic anchors. https://azoriginals.net/special-episode-on-building-strategic-anchors-the-table-group/

Now, take a look at *Fig 2-2. **The Way Forward**.* To download go to:

www.LTResults.com/monsterbook/resources

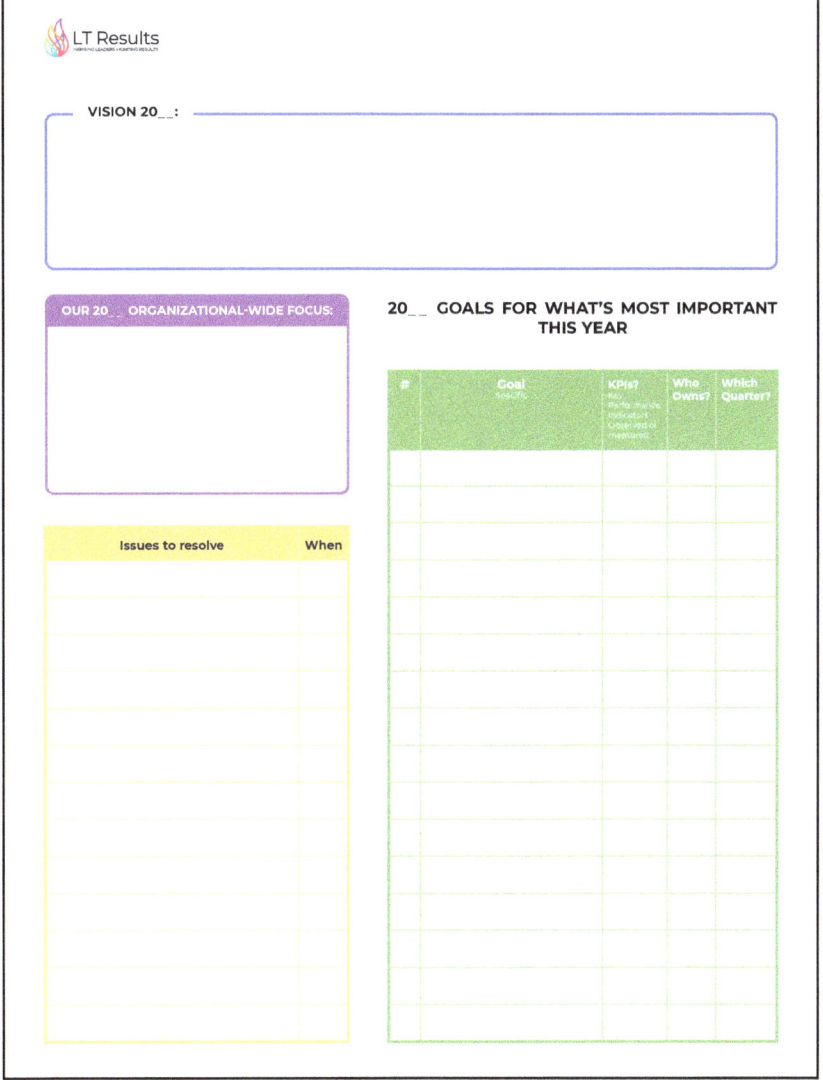

2023 Organizational-Wide Focus—The information you put here will also answer Question #5, "What is most important right now?"

If you wonder how to determine this, here is my recommendation. You and your team need to decide what will ultimately help your company realize its vision. This may not be easy, and the answer will be a company-wide goal for the year and focus everyone on accomplishing that goal. Crafting this all-important goal is often brainstormed in a workshop format where time is allowed to share, question, and challenge the concepts presented. The group then determines the number one choice and makes it the focus for the coming year.

Issues to Resolve—These are ongoing issues that you need to resolve at some point in the year to accomplish the organizational-wide focus. Target the quarter when you will address each issue, then cross them off the worksheet as you resolve them.

Goals for what's most important this year—You and your leadership team will create goals to accomplish the annual organizational focus. You will list actions to reach those goals. The description should be clear enough that someone outside the organization can mentally visualize what will occur. (Yes, I'm referring to SMART goals.)

SMART goals are:

Specific: Well-defined, clear, and unambiguous.

Measurable: With specific criteria that measure your progress.

Achievable: Attainable and not impossible to achieve.

Realistic: Within reach, realistic, and relevant to your purpose and vision.

<u>T</u>imely: With a clearly defined timeline, including a start and end dates, and in order to create urgency.

The "S" of SMART Goals—Specific

Goals that are specific have a greater chance of being accomplished. To make a goal specific, think through the answers and detail:

1. Who: Who is involved in this goal?
2. What: What do I want to accomplish?
3. Where: Where is this goal to be achieved?
4. When: When do I want to achieve this goal?
5. Why: Why do I want to achieve this goal?

The "M" of SMART Goals—Measurable

KPIs—Key Performance Indicators—are the **measurements** for a SMART goal. They are the criteria for measuring progress or how you will know if the goal is accomplished. What will be seen? Will there be a report, a meeting, or workshop? Will specific numbers in the business be tracked? Will something else happen that can be observed or measured? Tell us what you need to physically see to know the goal has been accomplished successfully.

The next column, "Who owns" refers to the individuals in the company who will be responsible and accountable for managing the goal and ensuring it is completed. That person may not do the actual work on the goal, but they have the ownership to report back on the status; it is their responsibility. (This answers Question # 6, "Who does what?")

The "T" of SMART Goals—Time-bound

For the last section, each goal has a time-definite stamp. The form requests the quarter of completion, but I suggest each quarter you break down the timing further to make this more specific and keep your team accountable to their commitments. Lastly, verify that the goal is **achievable** and **realistic**.

The "A" of SMART Goals—Achievable and Attainable

You should stretch a goal's achievability to make you feel challenged but define it well enough to actually achieve it. Ask yourself:

1. Do I have the resources and capabilities to achieve the goal? If not, what am I missing?
2. Have others done it successfully before?

The "R" of SMART Goals—Realistic

With the S, M, A, and T answered, the final check is:

1. Is the goal realistic?
2. Is the goal reachable, given the time and resources?

Many of my clients have completed these exercises, and I encourage you to do the same. You can be confident that you will put your business back on track. Completing these two forms alone (Fig. 2-1 and Fig. 2-2) will powerfully drive your business forward to achieve your company's vision and fulfill its mission.

Organizational Structure, Roles, and Responsibilities

If your business is 1) feeling stuck, 2) out of control, or 3) growing very fast, check out your roles and responsibilities list. Oops, you don't have one. We can fix that here. This is a vital tool to help your employees understand the larger picture of who does what and reports to whom.

In smaller businesses, we wear many hats, and we must perform all the roles ourselves.

That might look like this:

	Now:	**Future:**
	List the tasks that need to be done in the company by function. Then, ensure they are covered by someone, so that tasks don't fall through the cracks. Periodically re-evaluate the list to ensure tasks are covered.	Then, as the company continues to grow, hire individuals who best fit the function and can assume all tasks of that role. At this point, you may need to add more functional areas with new tasks. Follow the same process. Keep ensuring the tasks are being managed.

Here's an example of an ***Organizational Task & Accountability Chart***, *Fig 2-3*.

To download go to: www.LTResults.com/monsterbook/resources

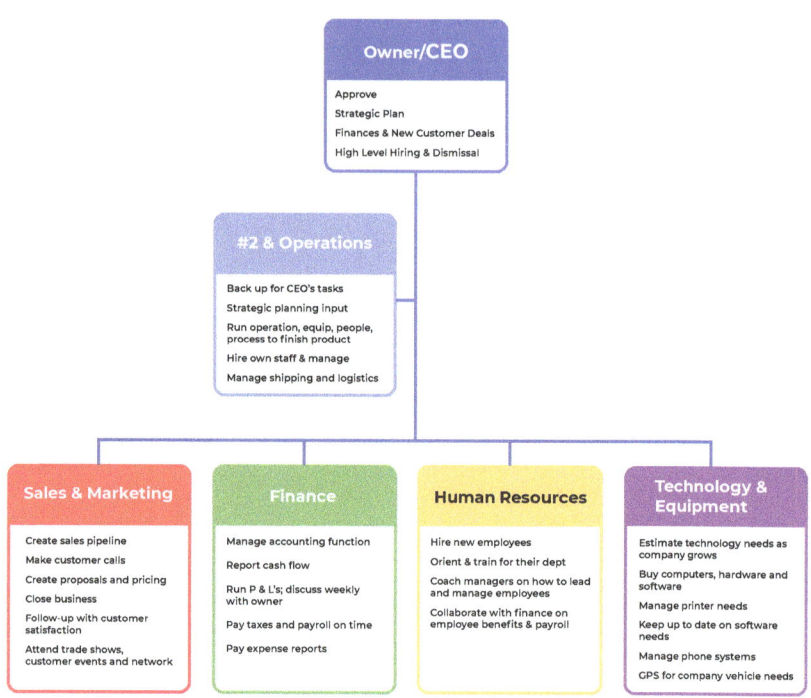

Here are some questions you may have:

"What happens if I'm the only one in my business?" When it is a one-person show, the owner does all the roles listed above.

When there are two or three people, you must decide who is accountable for which tasks to ensure nothing falls through the cracks. The coverage on the chart would change each time you hire additional staff.

Whether you have 100 or 1000+ people, this Organizational Task and Accountability chart will grow with you to accommodate additional roles. Simply add the category, list the tasks, and assign individuals to them. The chart scales up with you as the business matures.

 **Moment to Change**

From this chapter – Action Ideas:

1. Read or listen to Sinek, Simon, *Start with Why:* Portfolio, 2009, or his TED talk, https://www.youtube.com/watch?v=u4ZoJKF_VuA

2. Answer the Six Clarifying Questions for your business. Reference Lencioni, Patrick, *The Advantage: Why Organizational Health Trumps Everything Else in Business,* Jossey-Bass, 2012, and *Silos, Politics, and Turf Wars,* Jossey-Bass, 2008. There is a podcast specific to strategic anchors that you can find at: https://azoriginals.net/special-episode-on-building-strategic-anchors-the-table-group/

3. Fill in the Organizational Overview and The Way Forward forms in this book or download them from my website at www.LTResults.com/monsterbook/resources

4. Hold a company-wide meeting and communicate your vision and focus for the year using the forms as your guide.

5. Review your organization: Who does what? What are their talents? What does success look like if we carry out

our plans? Document your SMART goals into action plans.

6. Ensure your organization is clear about roles and responsibilities. Have you completed an Organizational Task & Accountability chart?

My dear leader – it is time to be honest regarding your strategy creation and implementation.

Are you more like Dr. Jekyll? 	Are you more like Mr. Hyde? 
• You have a purpose and vision written clearly with objectives and SMART goals that are being executed and updated? • Your organizational chart is clear. Tasks are assigned to individuals.	• No purpose or vision is written. No objectives or goals for this year are defined. You have no specific ideas for three, five, or ten years in the future. • No one is accountable for updating plans of action, there is no clear organizational structure, and no one is staying on top of projects.

Complete the following to inspire your moment to change. If you're like Dr. Jekyll, how could you improve further? If you're like Mr. Hyde, where do you need to start?

1. **What will I stop doing?**

2. What will I start doing?

3. What will I continue doing?

Spouse & Family's new comment,

> *"Thank goodness you started this business!"*

Please mark this chapter and come back to it. It is important to maintain a clear mission and vision throughout the life of your business. If things get off track, check your mission, vision, strategy, roles and responsibilities first—it will add clarity.

Who Am I? Clarifying and Linking Values and Beliefs

Your Spouse or Partner says:

> *"You don't keep your promises. You say you'll be here, but you aren't, so even if we don't go anywhere out of town, you can't even be home with us."*

Dear Leader, what grounds you?

Imagine for a moment that you are a hot air balloon. The wind is gently blowing and you are swaying from side to side, but not blowing away. What keeps you tethered? Are there several stakes that anchor you to the ground?

Now think about your life. What holds you firm to your truths and beliefs? Just like a hot air balloon, we require grounding to keep the strong winds of a crisis from blowing us off course. What keeps you in place? What guides you when strong winds blow?

In this chapter, we will examine the values that keep you anchored and guide you in your decision-making. We will also address blind spots that can occur when you are not tethered to consistent values and the unpredictable behaviors that may arise from such conditions.

Our values, beliefs, and attitudes are the moral principles that guide us in our lives and affect our behavior. We live our lives based on our core values. They are the foundation from where we make decisions. They ground us in strong winds.

Fig. 3-1, Beliefs and values drive behaviors

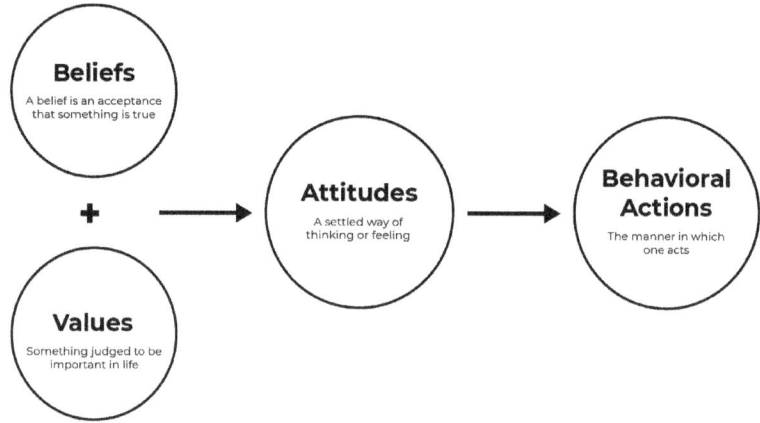

Beliefs are basically our convictions or assumptions about the world and how it works—such as "stealing is immoral." Beliefs are not something we can necessarily prove true. They grow from what we see, hear, experience, read, and think about. From these experiences, we develop opinions that we hold to be true and unmovable. As a result, we look for examples that prove our belief to be true.

Values are defined by the Oxford Dictionary as: "principles or standards of behavior; what we judge as important in life." They affect our attitudes and behavior. Our values are things we deem important, that drive us and motivate us to action. They guide our priorities. They also become the filter we use for decision-making. Values include honesty, faithfulness, respect, perseverance, and many other concepts.

Attitudes are feelings or opinions about something or someone that result in behavior. People primarily form their attitudes from underlying values and beliefs.

Behavioral actions then result as we act out our attitude regarding a situation or individual.

Our values and beliefs are not fixed. It is possible for them to change over time as we uncover evidence or have experiences that challenge our previously held views. They can also be strengthened by our experiences or evidence.

As a leader, people follow your words and your actions. Have you ever stopped to think about where your *right ways* of doing things originated? Do you have times when you think, "I sound just like my father," or "That's exactly what my mother used to say!" Right or wrong, we subconsciously operate off the values and beliefs demonstrated by our parents and those who raised us.

Let's look at our monsters for a minute to put this in context. An event or situation happens at work. The Dr. Jekyll in you would intentionally choose how to behave. You would know what you are doing and why. For example, it might be treating people with respect and kindness, —you were raised to believe that all people should be treated this way, regardless of the situation. Because of your upbringing you have a belief regarding respect for others and that became your personal value.

Conversely, as Mr. Hyde, in that same work situation, when the event occurs it *reminds you* of a past, traumatic experience. The Mr. Hyde in you yells at whomever is near. Your unconscious belief is that others may cause you harm and you must protect yourself. You've learned that yelling will keep people away from you so they will leave you alone. Your personal value then, may be to keep safe no matter what and yelling is how you do that.

I am not a therapist. There may be many deep-seated reasons why you or someone on your team behaves like Mr. Hyde. If that is the case, I encourage you to look to a cognitive behavioral therapist for support. A therapist can help a person sort through past events and give new ways to respond to unsettling situations. There is no judgment or shame in seeking help. What happens to individuals can be out of their control. Getting help to manage that behavior is within their control.

Where do those Mr. Hyde behaviors come from? If you look at Fig. 3-1 again, you'll see they come from what we value and what we believe, which feeds into our attitudes about a situation. Our attitude results in the behavioral actions that we take.

Fig. 3-1, Beliefs and values drive behaviors

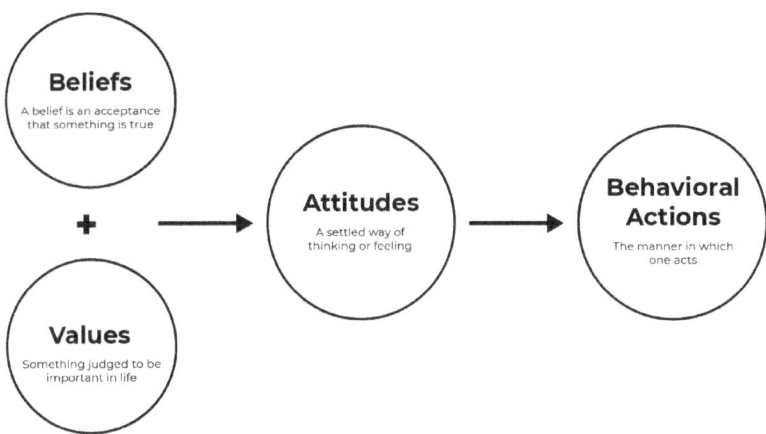

"When values, thoughts, feelings, and actions are in alignment, a person becomes focused and character is strengthened." — John C. Maxwell

Behavioral actions, like those of Dr. Jekyll or Mr. Hyde, can show up in your leadership role. To get to the root of those behaviors, let's explore the values that drive your beliefs.

A monster problem occurs in business when leaders are not aligned to their own core values. Because values are central to your decision-making, it's important to make sure your values are driven by you and not someone else.

"When your values are clear to you, making decisions becomes easier." — Roy E. Disney

For example, let's look at what happens in the office when you or one of your leaders behaves inconsistently with the value of being honest. In one instance, Eric is fired for lying to a customer about the timing of their order. He didn't want to look bad, the customer found out and was angry, and Eric was fired. In a different instance, Sallie lies to a customer about the timing of their order, but she's not fired. Why not? The order Sallie lied about was a very large dollar order and would have impacted the company's cash flow if the customer had become-dissatisfied and pulled the order. You supported Sallie's decision and made excuses to the customer to cover up the situation to protect the company's cash flow.

When your employee Sam questions you about the disparity in Eric and Sallie's situations, you feel he is challenging your authority and transform from kindly Dr. Jekyll to raging Mr. Hyde, exhibiting course, gruff, and discourteous reactions.

In this example, the values-based cliché "actions speak louder than words" shows up clearly. You need to be aware that you are probably having a values issue.

Here are other monster problems that arise from values-conflict issues:

- Lack of accountability within the staff. Staff appear to be hands-off and disengaged.

- Confused, indecisive staff.

- Fearful staff. They are afraid to come to you for decisions or tell you about decisions that were made in your absence.

- Toxic staff - Mr. Hyde-type behaviors in staff members, such as:

- Crude

- Abrupt

- Discourteous
- Inconsiderate
- Argumentative
- Questionably moral
- Inexplicably absent

Let's link back to our Eric and Sallie story and consider what caused a values issue to exist. You or other leaders inconsistently made decisions about who should be fired for lying. The value of honesty wasn't considered in the high-dollar scenario because the value of money outweighed it. Therefore, if you know that in your business cash could be more important than telling the truth, **don't** make honesty one of your core values.

The following are other possible ways this example might illustrate a values issue:

- Mr. Hyde behaviors showed up when questioned about your inconsistent decisions.
- Staff follow the way you or other leaders behave. They see what acceptable behavior looks like in your company.
- Everyone uses their own personal values to make decisions because there are no stated company values.
- Inconsistent decisions are made due to lack of defined decision-making criteria.

What would Dr. Jekyll look like in this scenario?

He would have done the internal personal work to understand what motivates him to action and fulfills him personally. Dr. Jekyll would know that he clearly articulates the values he wants to bring into the business. His values would include respect for others, curiosity and creativity, careful and objective observation of others, logic, and a slight skepticism and need for proof of accountability. He would have defined clear decision-making criteria to be used throughout his company based on the listed values.

There is a Netflix series titled, "Better Call Saul." In it there is a scene where Saul thinks about starting his own business. He wants his girlfriend, Kim, to join the business. She's very ethical and abides by the law. Saul, on the other hand, has a more creative approach to lawyering. However, he wants Kim to be part of his company. He internally struggles between two things: 1) Does he lie about who he is and how he's going to run his business to get Kim to join him, or 2) Does he remain true to who he really because it is his business?

In the show, you see the mental struggle on his face until finally he says, "No luck, this is who I am, and this is how I'm going to run my business." Kim does not join him. However, they find a resolution. They simply share office space, and each runs their own company based on their own values.

The moral of the story is this. If you believe one way and behave another, it will eventually result in an internal struggle, both mentally and physically. It could turn into burnout, show up as disease, or create conflicts in your personal life. All because you are not true to your values, and people see you say one thing and act another way.

Through the years, I have used multiple exercises in client organizations to discern organizational values. Below are a couple of simple ones. I recommend you start with the values of the owners and key leader(s) to define the company's values.

1. Think about the people who have been fired from the company in the past. Why were they fired? Write down those reasons and notice any patterns that emerge. Most likely the answers will reveal the values that the owner and leader(s) hold dear and have been the unstated values of the company. Now you can clearly list those for going forward.

2. If want to test another way, owners and leaders can think about someone who has offended them. Which of their values were violated? List those.

While living in Asia, I completed a Self-Managing Leadership program with Brahma Kumari's Academy for a Better World. We spent time reflecting and understanding our core beliefs. The following worksheet, Fig. 3-2 , was one of the most helpful tools for uncovering my personal values. Try it out for yourself.

Fig. 3-2, Values Most Deeply Connected to Your Purpose in Life,

to download go to: www.LTResults.com/monsterbook/resources

LT Results

THE VALUES MOST DEEPLY CONNECTED TO YOUR PURPOSE IN LIFE

These are the basis for all your important choices and decisions in the future:

Bring into your mind the image of a favorite hero or heroine. Heroes may be real or imaginary figures who inspire you. What particular 1 or 2 qualities do they possess that appeal to you?	What would you be prepered to die for?
Bring into your mind a favorite poem, piece or literature, or song. What particular 1 or 2 qualities does it reflect that you like?	What are you prepared to live for?
Think of a time when you felt very proud of yourself for a taking a stand on an issue that was important to you. What were the values you were protecting at that time?	The values that will influece my choices, decisions, and guide my behavior in the next chapter or my life are:

Copyright © Brahma Kumaris Academy for a Better World

The answers from your worksheet represent your values and are most likely your core decision-making criteria, too. Are the values you've uncovered the same ones you expect your employees to follow? Or do you expect different values than the ones you identified?

If you are the key decision-maker, ensure the values selected align with your personal values, or at some point you will experience a disconnect and dissatisfaction in your business.

Organizational values are important because:

1. They drive employees to work towards a purpose. **Engaged** employees usually have values that are aligned with their organization's values.

2. They are specific and actionable, and link to your rewards and recognition systems.

3. They define your company culture and the behavior expected.

TO DO:

Return to your Strategic Planning form from Chapter 2, *fig. 2-1, Organizational Overview,* and record your company values on that page. Remember these will drive your decision-making.

MOTIVATING DRIVERS:

Motivating drivers are the reasons we get out of bed in the morning. Connecting to them allows you to be personally and professionally engaged and fulfilled. If you understand your motivating drivers and those of your employees, you can truly connect to what matters to your team members. You will be able to ensure they are also engaged and fulfilled in their roles, and thus create a higher performing company.

How does a leader acquire this vital information regarding what motivates an employee? In my years of consulting I have found a shortcut that I believe can benefit any business: online assessments. I prefer assessments by Target Training International (TTI). This global organization has a research-based background that validates each assessment they create. TTI averages 86-93% accuracy in their reporting. I have been an assessment provider with TTI for over 20 years. They continue to keep their tools relevant and backed by research and patents.

Motivating Driver online assessments allow employees, and other individuals, to answer questions in a place they feel at ease. The results are immediately presented back to the employee in the form of customized reports. The reports describe and rank their motivating drivers in priority order. These motivating drivers encompass traits like resourcefulness, harmony, power, serving the greater good, serving themselves, seeking knowledge, or collaboration. Once assessment providers explain the results to employees, leaders usually see rapid buy-in and accountability. The reports give individuals objective feedback and make it easier for a leader to coach and develop these assessed employees.

If you want to learn more about what motivates you and your team, turn to Chapter 10 – Quick Reference & Resources, to contact me.

WHAT IF?

What if you find you have staff who don't align with your values? What do you do? They will either naturally align and understand why your company exists, or they will self-select out and move to a company that better fits their personal values. However, while such staff remain in your company, communicate your expectations clearly and hold them to your expressed company values.

 **Moment to Change**

Am I like Dr. Jekyll? 	Am I like Mr. Hyde?
• I am clear where my beliefs come from and consciously choose them. • I am guided by my personal values and have established core operating values for my organization. • I use my values as decision-making criteria.	• I have not taken the time to reflect on the origin of my beliefs or defined my personal or company values. • I am upset by some situations or attitudes of others and react unprofessionally at times. • My actions speak louder than my words, and instead say, "Do as I say not as I do."

Ideas for how to become more like Dr. Jekyll:

- Return to your Strategic Planning form from Chapter 2, fig. 2-1, Organizational Overview. Record your company values on that page. Remember these will drive your decision-making.

- Review the source of your values and beliefs. As you see in our Chapter 3 monster picture, you may have many voices speaking in your head. Who's really leading?

- Answer the questions about who you've fired and fill in the worksheet to determine your values.

- Reference Chapter 10 – Quick Reference & Resources to access online assessments to identify your personal motivating drivers.

Regardless of if you're Mr. Jekyll-like or Mr. Hyde-like, what else can you do?

1. **What can I start doing?**
2. **What can I stop doing?**
3. **What can I continue doing?**

Anything you can do to know yourself better and understand your "why" will only make you and your business better. It will positively impact those around you, especially your family. It takes courage to take that step, but if you're running your own company, and reading this book, you've already proven that you have courage and are willing to make a difference in the world.

"Keep your thoughts positive because your thoughts become your words.
Keep your words positive because your words become your behavior.
Keep your behavior positive because your behavior

becomes your habits. Keep your habits positive because your habits become your values. Keep your values positive because your values become your destiny." — Mahatma Ghandi

Your spouse or partner now says:

> *"Thank you for keeping your promises. We know we can always count on you to do what you say you will do."*

Do I show I care?
Understand and Engage Others

Dear Leader, Have you had time to clarify your values? If so, you may already have experienced quicker decision-making and a company culture that reflects your values with a new way of working. In this chapter, we will deepen your values as we explore how leaders show care and engage others.

Have you heard any of the following statements from your spouse or partner?

> *"Do you even think about me or the children when you make your plans? Let me remind you that during the pandemic we were all on lockdown and you acted like nothing was wrong and left us to go to work! We were scared to death to go pick up groceries! The kids weren't going to school. Someone had to stay home with OUR children and teach them! Guess who had to do that?ME, my career had to go on hold. Not yours."*

If you have, stay tuned. This chapter will help you relate better to your family, friends, customers, employees, and others—*and* make everything and everyone you touch a little bit better. Let's start with the definition of caring.

Merriam-Webster's dictionary defines *Caring* as, "feeling or showing concert for or kindness to another." As leaders we need to display caring to our staff, customers, employees, and others to inspire them to their best. What does that entail?

To display caring is to conspicuously demonstrate a quality, emotion, or skill. You can't just say you care; you need to show it. That's what truly makes the difference in both professional and personal relationships.

We aren't all gifted when it comes to showing care and compassion. But I've met many leaders who are able to display these actions. The rest of us may empathize with a person's situation—mentally understand and imagine their feelings or experience—but have to work harder to physically display our concern.

Remember the difference this way: Care is driven with the heart and displays actions of kindness and concern for others, whereas empathy is driven with the head and understands and acknowledges an emotion or situation from a mental distance. A successful Dr. Jekyll leader must balance when to show empathy or caring, while ensuring the work gets done.

Let's explore what I mean with an example. The Covid-19 pandemic is a scenario that everyone can relate to in some way. I realize that for some this memory may set off other emotions. That is the point of this reflection. Everyone experienced the pandemic, with their own reactions, from leader to employee to family member. Now, think back to March 2020, the very start of the "shutdown" (internationally, January or February 2020). Reflect on the following:

- How did you behave as an owner, executive, or manager?

- How did you react if a shutdown for your business was suggested or demanded?

- What were your reactions as a son or daughter, offspring, or sibling?

- How did you manage things with grandparents or other elderly family members?

- What about as a partner or spouse?

- If you're a parent, how did you respond to your children?

- How did you respond as community or church leader? As a public official?

As you think back, how did you demonstrate caring in these situations? What did it look like? Was it different for each situation?

- Did you go home to be with your parents or your family members?

- Did you stay on-site to be sure all your employees were safe and the facility was locked down?

- Did you stay at the office even when all others went home to care for their friends, families, neighbors, church members, or pets?

What kind of caring did you exhibit in those various roles?

To help you understand how caring can appear at different levels, look at the following model developed by Abraham Maslow:

Maslow's Hierarchy of Needs. This model details how caring presents in different situations. First, the background on the model.

Fig. 4-1 the Theory of Needs

From Featured Masterclass Instructor, Robin Arzón:

In a 1943 paper titled "A Theory of Human Motivation," American psychologist Abraham Maslow theorized that human decision-making is undergirded by a hierarchy of psychological needs. In his initial paper and a subsequent 1954 book titled Motivation and Personality, Maslow proposed that five core needs form the basis for human behavioral motivation.

Maslow referred to self-actualization as a "growth need," and he separated it from the lower four levels on his hierarchy, which he called "deficiency needs."

According to his theory, if you fail to meet your deficiency needs, you'll experience harmful or unpleasant results. Conditions ranging from illness and starvation up through loneliness and self-doubt are the byproduct of unmet deficiency needs.

By contrast, self-actualization needs can make you happier, but you are not harmed when these needs go unfulfilled. Thus, self-actualization needs only become a priority when the other four foundational needs are met first.

Fig. 4-2: Maslow's Hierarchy of Needs

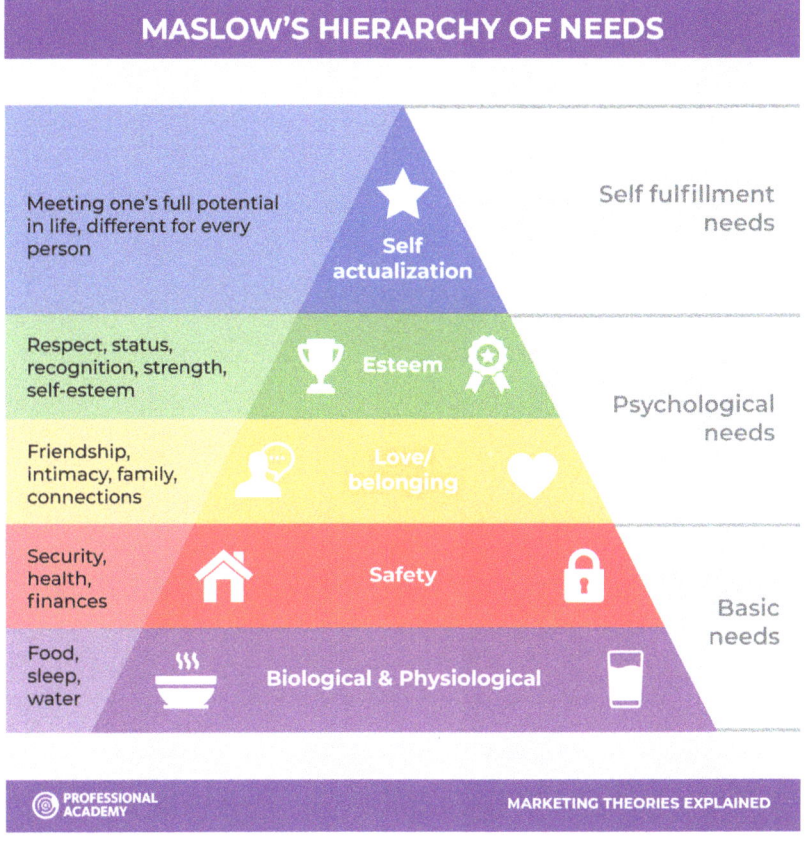

Adapted to US English

"Too often we underestimate the power of a touch, a smile, a kind word, a listening ear, an honest compliment, or the smallest act of caring, all of which have the potential to turn a life around."— Leo F. Buscaglia

Maslow's Hierarchy of Needs (Fig. 4-2) illustrates needs in three distinct categories. Those are: Basic Needs, Psychological Needs, and Self-fulfillment Needs. Maslow's theory says one does not move out of a level until its needs are satisfied. Once they are, the person moves up to the next level. Let's start at the bottom of the pyramid. The first Basic need is: 1) Biological & Physiological Needs, which are things like food, water, and sleep. The second is: 2) Safety Needs, which are things like security, finances, and health.

The next category on the pyramid is Psychological Needs. Those needs are 3) Love and Belonging, which include friendship, intimacy, family, and connections, and 4) Esteem needs, which are respect, status, recognition, strength, and self-esteem.

At the top of the pyramid is Self-actualization. These self-fulfillment needs are different for every person. Self-actualized individuals are happy, live their talents, and fully express themselves. As Maslow stated , *self-actualization needs only become a priority when the other four foundational needs are met first.* This is the pinnacle of the pyramid.

Let's think again about our example of the COVID-19 pandemic. A government entity may have directed you to shut down your business for a period of time. If you were an *essential* business, you had the option to stay open but had to incorporate strict safety guidelines and physically change the workspace to distance individuals six feet apart (1.82 m). This was a first-time occurrence in the U.S., and in many parts of the world. We all operated in a way never experienced before. Whether from government, nonprofit, or private sectors, leaders were not sure what would work or not. Many people lived in a constant state of fear and panic and did not feel safe. They remained at level 2, because their safety needs were unmet.

Look at the chart again, and let's connect this more closely to your experience. Where were you on the chart in March 2020? Were you concerned about your most basic needs? Were they Physiological, or higher up the pyramid?

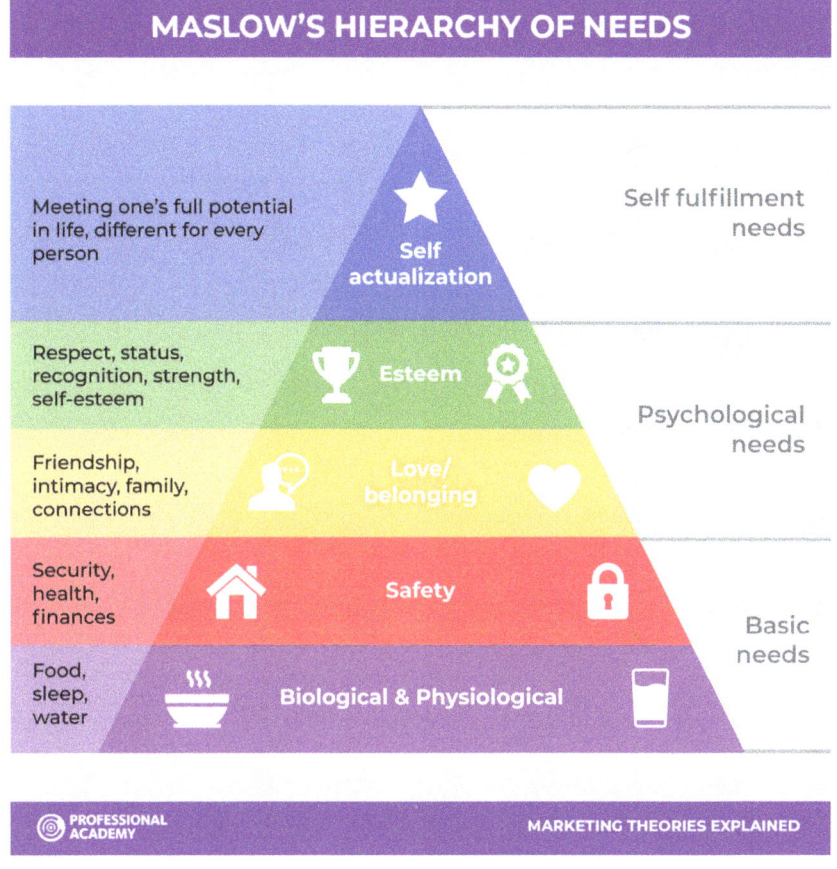

Adapted to US English

Where do you think your spouse or partner was at that time? Your children? Siblings? Parents? Other coworkers? If you've never asked how others felt, have that conversation now. Listen to where they were both mentally and physically. You will help these individuals move up the pyramid as you display care and compassion by listening.

Do you recall during shutdown how everyone rushed to grocery stores to buy toilet paper, tissues, and paper towels? As the grocery store shelves emptied, people panicked. Some still grabbed water and food, while others moved up to the next level and purchase safety and security items like masks, locks, propane, guns, and ammunition.

Many worked from home virtually. That same technology allowed people to visually connect again with coworkers, have after-hour chats with family, and host video cocktail parties with friends. Families created game nights and played board games together. People came out on balconies to sing together. There was connection and belonging, and individuals moved up another level in the hierarchy by meeting the Psychological needs of Love and Belonging.

After the belonging need was satisfied, individuals moved on to their Esteem needs. Some figured out new innovations and ways to help others. They were viewed as heroes in their communities. As a society, we cheered on medical workers and recognized medical personnel for the sacrifices they made. In other situations, people used their talents to make and distribute masks, while some served quarantined or home-bound individuals. All these actions fulfilled Esteem needs as identified in Maslow's hierarchy.

Once individuals satisfied their esteem needs, some evolved to Self-actualization. Individuals had confidence to fully express themselves, their talents, and their ideas. They strived to be in the moment and make the world a better place. Musicians played to take our minds and souls away from fear and provide comfort through their music. People who were Self-actualized felt joy and happiness, due to an internal knowing that they were fulfilling their life's purpose. They were at the pinnacle of Maslow's Pyramid.

Dear Leader, if you were a Mr. Hyde at that moment, your actions may have been something like this during the height of the pandemic: You worked at your office to get a spreadsheet completed and needed immediate assistance to meet your deadline. You called your accountant, Chris, who was supposed to be working from home. On the call you immediately jumped into business questions without asking how they were doing. Chris told you they could not help you at that moment as they were dealing with some personal issues with no other explanation. You were miffed and became angry and hung up, thinking how all your employees have taken advantage of your company during this pandemic. The accountant's lower-level needs were dominant. Chris couldn't address your task until their Basic needs were satisfied.

Could that scenario have been different if you had shown your accountant concern up front? Let's see how a Dr. Jekyll leader would have managed the same situation.

Dr. Jekyll first asked Chris how they were doing only to find out that their father-in-law was in the hospital with COVID-19, and their spouse was on the phone with doctors at that moment, while Chris was managing the children and their online school. Dr. Jekyll would have acknowledged these statements and apologized for disturbing them. The accountant knew they were to have been working and asked Dr. Jekyll to hold while they answered a child's question. Dr. Jekyll kindly agreed. When Chris came back to the phone, they asked Dr. Jekyll why he called. Dr. Jekyll said he had a deadline and needed some back up financials. Chris told Dr. Jekyll where to find the file to answer his questions to meet his deadline.

In this instance, the caring tone that Dr. Jekyll portrayed to the accountant and the time he allowed them to tend to the children, allowed Chris to address their lower-level pyramid needs for their family and move up to esteem where they could professionally assist with Dr. Jekyll's request.

How many employees during the pandemic were not able to give you what you were asking of them? Did you recognize that their lower-level needs were screaming at them? Those employees felt it crucial to ensure that they and their families were physically and mentally safe first, and they couldn't concentrate on anything else until that had occurred.

If, at that moment, you didn't understand, you may have been agitated and sounded gruff to those employees. I heard many leaders blame employee problems on the "virtual" environment rather than recognize that they, as the leader, requested assistance and approached employees with a lack of care and concern for what was occurring in the world.

Please understand, I'm writing this as much for me as I am for you. Many of us get so involved in our own "stuff" that we can't see or help others with theirs. However, if we stop to listen, show caring, and understand their level of need, they will be more likely to help us. We are then modeling the behavior we'd like to have from others.

Communication flows more easily and trust is built when positive interpersonal relationships are developed between employees and management. Such exchanges help employees feel more comfortable with management, and the result is enhanced employee satisfaction, improved work ethic, and increased employee engagement because they are happy with their role in the company. Leaders should aim to reinforce how much they value communication with staff.

Understanding and using Maslow's Hierarchy of Needs will provide you with an excellent tool to build trust.

Fig. 4-3, How to Show Care using Maslow's Hierarchy of Needs

How it applies to	Physiological Needs	Safety	Love/Belonging	Esteem	Self Actualization
Yourself	You need air, food, water, shelter, sleep, warmth.	Stay alert and be aware of your surroundings. Give the impression that you are calm, confident, and know where you are going. Trust your instincts. If it doesn't look or feel right, it might not be.	Be mindful of others. Make the other person your focus. Keep and teach an open mind. Practice an attitude of acceptance and appreciation. Invite others to join. Join others. Ask for support.	Be kind to yourself. Recognize and challenge your unkind thoughts. Focus on the positives. Learn to assert yourself. Do things you enjoy. Push self to show confidence. Try something new.	Live to your full potential; express your natural gifts. Practice acceptance. Live life as it comes. Live spontaneously. Live authentically. Be all you can be. Accept yourself fully.
Your family	They need groceries, water, a place to sleep and stay warm or cool.	Security needs include safety, shelter, security, law & order, employment, health, stability. Provide home security and transportation. Be ready to administer first aid. Prevent household poisonings. Be prepared for emergencies. Get rid of tripping hazards.	Social needs, include belonging, love, affection, intimacy, family, friends, relationships. Attend to important relationships. Take time. Be present. Express Appreciation. Listen. Learn to communicate. Apologize and forgive. Attend to the communities where we belong.	Appreciate your children. Guide them toward their strengths. Encourage their confidence & courage. Attend family activities; recognize achievements. Appreciate & thank your parents/grandparents.	Allow spouse and family members opportunities for self-expression and expansion. Time to be alone to use and explore their talents and gifts. If talents not yet discovered, encourage trying new things until they do. Don't limit interests; some have many talents to express.
Your support team or staff	They need access to a restroom, a place to get drinking water, breaks to eat meals and snacks, and a comfortable working environment.	Protect employees from work-related illness and injury and make the workplace (building, etc) secure from intruders. Every company should have a workplace safety plan (Environmental, Safety, and Health Policy statement).	Check in with people. Give people the floor who are feeling ignored. Celebrate Self-identity. Ask for input. Encourage Employee-led Communities.	Encourage learning. Provide opportunities for additional training. Recognize others' knowledge and skills personally & professionally. Provide challenging projects. Publicly & privately recognize accomplishments and effort.	Encourage employees to use natural talents for personal & professional fulfillment. Hire individuals aligned to company's values and vision to match their "whys." A company's path to self-actualization is through its employees' expression of theirs.
Your customers	If your customers are on site, they need access to a restroom, a place to get drinking water, and a comfortable environment.	Provide a safe experience while making a purchase or while waiting for a service to be completed. Many types of safety policies can be put in place to ensure that customers are kept safe during a business transaction.	Introduce your customers to each other. Remember something about them. Send thank you notes or gifts of appreciation. Assign them a contact person to feel part of the team. Ask for testimonials and put on website.	Hold customer appreciation days. Ensure a company culture of follow-through & customer satisfaction. Spotlight "a customer of the month" on website. Include customer examples in company blog or newsletter. Offer to provide testimonials for their websites.	Help key decision-makers be all they can be. Provide services that enable clients to be even better in their business. Find opportunities to support customers' causes and beliefs. Target customers who align to your beliefs to help both companies self-actualize.

You still may not be convinced if you are asking yourself, "Why should I really care? What does it have to do with my business?"

Dr. Jekyll behaviors show us that there are increased and improved organizational benefits when we behave in a kindly, professional manner, with strong, caring communication.

Effective communication impacts organizational success because it:

- Gives employees a voice—you understand their need for esteem and respect; they become more engaged and committed to your company and its causes.

- Builds employee morale and satisfaction.

- Helps employees understand your expectations and talk about their ability to meet those expectations.

- Helps reduce misunderstandings, grievances, and even lawsuits.

- Improves processes and procedures and ultimately creates greater efficiencies and reduced costs.

- Unites your team to work more effectively together and productively.

- Builds a company's culture (culture is the characteristic features of everyday existence shared by people in a place or time).

There are many Mr. Hyde behaviors. If you recognize some in yourself, it doesn't mean you are a monster. But during a poor communication exchange, it may feel that way to others, even if it is unintentional. If you wish to achieve the impact you desire, it is vital to understand that **how** you communicate is as important as the message you intend to deliver.

A Google search can reveal specific steps for how to communicate in any situation. However, if you will memorize and practice the following timeless **Basic Principles**, originally created by Zenger-Miller in 1986, you will never show up as Mr. Hyde again and will always be regarded as a professional Dr. Jekyll.

Fig. 4-4, The Basic Principles

Basic Principles

1. Focus on the situation, issue, or behavior, not on the person.
2. Maintain the self-confidence and self-esteem of others.
3. Maintain constructive relationships with your employees, peers, and managers.
4. Take initiative to make things better.
5. Lead by example.

Copyright © 1986 by Zenger-Miller

I speak from experience. My very dear, long-term friend, and mentor, Marilyn (Hornick) Kobb knew and lived these principles. I once heard Marilyn deliver these Basic Principles to a group of supervisors and managers.

I recall Marilyn's response in the workshop when finger-pointing or conflict arose. Time after time, she used the Basic Principles to resolve such situations. She would pause the training and,

1. calmly clarify the real issue that had upset the opposing managers. She would then

2. give each time to air their views. If the views were negative, she would note that as leaders they should

3. find ways to make things better, not just complain. Marilyn would

4. ask the leaders to come up with ideas to resolve the issue or improve the situation. In one case she suggested that they take their suggestions and ideas to the Regional Operations Director, who had a reputation of being a "strict," no-nonsense individual, with extremely high standards, to (4 & 5) champion the issue being resolved.

The managers listened and bought into the steps until she said, "Present it to the Regional Operations Director," and at that point their mouths dropped open with shock and horror! She then,

5. lead by example. Marilyn offered to go with the managers to meet the Regional Operations Director and ensure their views were heard. Ultimately, Marilyn

6. maintained constructive relationships for all.

Those are the skills of a pro. They are simple and direct. Effective communication and leadership do not have to be complicated!

The effects of improved communication may not appear overnight. I recommend:

1. Stick with it for the long haul, and eventually your business will reap the rewards of better communication in the workplace.

2. Check in with a business peer or mentor whenever possible to talk about how things are going and to brainstorm ways to continue to improve communication between you, your employees, customers, and vendors.

As a leader, your role in caring communication is to inform and at times, INSPIRE. It's vital to your business that your communication efforts inspire your team as much as they exhibit caring and direction. Plan for meetings and conversations. Effectively mix information and inspiration.

John Eades, author, Podcaster, and CEO of Learnlof reinforced this in an *INC* article dated April 29, 2019, "3 Ways to Immediately Inspire Anybody (From the Moment You Meet Them) Inspiration is a Critical Element to Being a Successful Leader."

When you inspire others, you motivate them to do their best work, set higher goals for themselves and achieve more. Becoming a truly inspirational leader, you will gain the respect of employees and others, lifting everyone around you so that everyone can achieve greater results. Here are three ways to be a more inspirational leader:

1. Demonstrate enthusiasm and vision.

Great leaders fully believe in their company's mission (purpose) and work tirelessly to communicate their vision to others. They display a type of enthusiasm and passion that is often referred to in psychology as "zest."

Truly inspirational leaders bring this same type of enthusiasm to their everyday work, leveraging it as a powerful motivating factor that helps others become more engaged and committed to what they do. **The key is that your zest and enthusiasm must be authentic.**

2. Show you care.

One of the best ways to ensure that your enthusiasm in the workplace comes off as genuine is to simultaneously demonstrate that you care about those you lead. While it might seem obvious, many leaders share only their competence and expertise, and forget to show others they genuinely care.

Take time out to speak with different people in your organization. Ask questions and truly listen so you can better understand their needs and how to reach them. Don't be afraid to ask about what is going on in their life, both inside and outside of work.

3. Inspire by action.

Inspiring leaders don't just talk the talk. They also walk the walk. They live out that definition of a leader by focusing on their actions and their example.

Consistently giving your best effort and following through on expectations and promises will inspire others to do the same.

*Try the **PTS Method**. It short for **Prepare to Serve**. Anytime you change environments, say to yourself "Prepare to Serve." This technique will have you focused on your actions and examples with much more thought.*

Truly inspiring leaders understand that what they do ultimately matters far more than what they say. As you consistently follow these three steps in your interactions with others, you will serve as a lasting inspirational influence who helps others achieve greater outcomes.

All too often, we are moving so fast we don't slow down to be able to "go fast." Think ahead about **what** needs to be communicated, **how** it should be communicated, **who** it should be communicated to, and **when** it should be communicated to use your time wisely and impact your business significantly.

"Your ability to communicate with others will account for fully 85% of your success in your business and in your life." —Brian Tracy, motivational speaker

85% success! That's a number worth shooting for. Please take an opportunity to improve your personal communication skills and thus enhance your business.

 **Moment to Change**

In this chapter we've covered:

1. Maslow's Hierarchy of Needs and how to apply it to spouses, family, employees, teams, and customers to show you care.

2. The impact of communication on your business, and how to communicate using the Basic Principles.

3. Steps to inspire others.

Am I Dr. Jekyll?	Am I Mr. Hyde?
If you are already doing much of this, write down what else you may be able to start, stop, and continue doing below. An idea might be to coach or mentor a Mr. Hyde who's on your team.	If you feel you or others on your team may be showing up like Mr. Hyde, fill in what you can start, stop, and continue doing.

1. **What will you start doing?**

2. **What will you stop doing?**

3. **There is always something done well – what will you continue doing in terms of caring for or communicating with others?**

"To be successful is to be helpful, caring and construc-tive, to make everything and everyone you touch a little bit better."—Norman Vincent Peale

You now say:

> *"Honey, I'm going to take a couple of days off. Do you want me to take the kids somewhere so you can have some quiet time to focus on your work?"*

In the next chapter, we will identify the chaos-creators. Join me there to get your organization performing at an even higher level than it is today.

CHAPTER 5

Am I a Chaos-Creator? Top Business Processes to Restore Calm

Welcome back Leader! The last chapter covered how to understand other people's needs, how to demonstrate caring communication, and how to inspire others to action.

In this chapter, we will explore what happens when there is chaos in a business or organization. You are dealing with chaos when you hear any of these statements from your spouse or partner:

> *"When you are here, you are not mentally here. You're on your phone, computer, or tablet at all hours of the day and night, not even putting it down on weekends."*
>
> *"You can't seem to make a decision and stick to it. One moment you decide and then you take it back the next moment."*
>
> *"You hire all these people and then you don't even let them run the company. You have to be involved in everything!"*

Merriam-Webster's dictionary defines **Chaos** as, "a state of utter confusion."

Part of owning a business is managing the constant battle between chaos and stability. It is a fine balance that often leans more toward chaos than stability. What causes chaos? Chaos occurs when a leader is unclear about what to correct and/or how to correct it. There is such a thing as *managed chaos*, in which a situation *appears* to be completely disorganized but actually operates with key functions under control. An organization can operate positively in managed chaos. To be clear, for our purposes I will use the term chaos for an out-of-control situation that has negative effects on you and the members of your team.

In my experience, it is easier to spot chaos in small and midsize businesses, but it exists in larger organizations as well. In larger businesses, it is easier for people and projects to hide (Hyde) but you can be assured that they are still there. Dear Leader, we are about to hunt for chaos in *your* business, so as we go forward use your own business situation for context, whatever your role. Your workplace is where I would like you to focus.

Think back to a situation where utter confusion occurred among your employees or team members. They didn't know what project or task to work on, people blamed others for dropping the ball, and everyone seemed overwhelmed. Key decisions had not been made, and so products or services were delayed due to lack of materials, instructions, or people to do the work. As a result, an important customer had called to complain. She was tired of waiting and nearly exploded with anger. You hadn't fulfilled your agreement with your customer.

UGH! Not even a memory you want to have, right? Please mentally remain in that disorganized pain just a bit longer to help me make this next point. Did you ever discover what made the whole thing unravel? Were you in the office or area when it happened? Was one person to blame? Was the situation resolved or have you not had time to deal with it?

Think about Mr. Hyde for a moment. He disrupts. He is unpredictable. He is overcontrolling or overbearing. He doesn't take responsibility for anything except a role in scaring or blaming others. His emotions are erratic. One moment he may be angry, another frustrated, and yet another domineering.

Now compare the chaos situation you were thinking about with the actions of Mr. Hyde. Could he have been the manager in your situation?

Back to my original question—What causes **chaos**?

- Lack of processes by which the company operates.
- An overcontrolling leader.
- An *under* controlling leader who doesn't know how to prioritize work or tasks.
- Confused team members who don't know what's considered a priority, so they pick the easiest task or the task they like best.
- Lack of staff.
- Fear of hiring staff.
- Busyness—You do tasks yourself and do not delegate so you can focus on managing your business.
- Unclear responsibilities—People blaming one another.
- Lack of accountability.

- Lack of focus and priority—Everything needs to be done, NOW.

As leaders we can hide many things. Inevitably though, these hidden secrets will leak out in the form of chaos. Think about your team. If any of the above list occurs in your workplace, your employees probably feel burned out, not cared for, or not valued for what they do. There is likely little camaraderie, and people don't trust each other. Possibly the only "fun" that occurs is *poking fun* at others in a harmful or sarcastic way. People are most likely fed up and irritable.

If any of that has happened, you can bet there is some verbal complaining going on in the workplace. What do you think your customers have overheard? Even if your employees believe they watch their words, you can bet others will pick up on their dissatisfied comments and tone of voice. Have you recently called your office to hear for yourself what may be going on in the background? My guess is that from time-to-time your customers may have heard:

Irritable people who do not listen or who are rude to one another.

Employees who blame others in the company or suppliers outside as the cause of late or missed deliveries.

When your customers hear those things, they may:

Become irritable themselves (even if they were not irritated when they called).

Gain an immediate impression that your company is a zoo. Or worse, they decide not to do business with you because of what they heard.

Those are only *two* of the things that could happen!

It can feel overwhelming in a moment like one of the above scenarios, whether you are the boss or an employee. Remember Maslow's hierarchy of needs from the last chapter? Where are your needs on the pyramid at that moment? Where are those of your employees? Your customers? We all have different life experiences that influence us in the background; as a result, we will each react differently to the same situation.

When you feel overwhelmed and tired, your Mr. Hyde may show up. Even your employees may exhibit some Mr. Hyde behaviors! In some cases, Mr. Hyde-types just plain hide; no one can find them. Take heart, I'll break down those chaos-creators next and show you what's behind each.

To do that, think of our scientist, Dr. Jekyll. In my mind, scientists are logical, thoughtful, and detail-focused. Would you agree with me that our Dr. Jekyll is organized and systematic? He has an affinity for being process-driven, which means he knows that Task A has to occur first so that Task B, then C, can be completed.

Top Chaos-Creator: Lack of documented processes

Let's apply that Dr. Jekyll scientific thinking to situations at your company. Leader, do you know the top ten key processes for your company?

YES   or   NO   are your only choices, pick one.

Let me explain why defined key processes are critical if you wish to eliminate chaos in your business.

- When you're not present, people know what to do in your absence and remain productive.

- Everything that is done in your business is consistent. Consistence can improve quality.

- When one person is away, someone else can step in and pick up their task. People resources are focused and productive.

- Time and money are both saved. Employees do not wander and waste time on the clock.

- Customer service is improved, which can result in increased sales, thanks to happier customers.

- Employees are less frustrated and know what is expected of them. That can improve your company culture because they understand their roles and know how to perform their work.

Have I convinced you that documented processes are important to have?　　YES!　　(Thanks for agreeing!)

What are the processes?

There are specific processes in your organization that make it unique. That uniqueness needs to be documented. It's what some companies refer to as *their secret sauce*, while others use the phrase, *"Your 3 Uniques."* It's what sets you apart from the competition. Think about your business:

Your *secret sauce* is these items that you do differently than your competition:

-
-
-

Your Actions:

Work with your team to define what you do differently from the competition that makes you unique.

Have the team write out your secret sauce process steps to make it repeatable (also referred to as scalable) and part of who you are.

There are also standard business processes that allow a company to run smoothly and efficiently; without them there is chaos. The following are questions **to ask yourself** about your own standard business processes. Make your notes here to come back and act on later.

Fig. 5-1, List of Questions to Ask Yourself about Your Top Business Processes:

Decision-Making Processes:

☐ Do we have a company decision-making process?

☐ Are our decisions in line with our values from Chapter 3?

☐ How do we make decisions for situations that cost ($X)? For example, $2,000 dollars or under?

☐ Who is authorized to do this?

☐ How do we make decisions for situations that cost ($X)? Following the same example, $2,000 and over?

☐ Who is authorized to do this?

☐ Is our chain of command documented?

☐ When the owner is out, who is next in charge?

Employment Processes:

- ☐ What are our steps to hire employees?
- ☐ What are our steps to be fired?
- ☐ Are our processes in line with our values from Chapter 3?
- ☐ Do we know why or when we hire people?
- ☐ Do we know why or when we fire people?
- ☐ Do we have documented processes for orientation to the organization?

Manage Performance Processes: Once we have an employee on board, how do we manage their performance?

- ☐ Do we set expectations?
  - o How?
  - o When?

- ☐ Do we coach to expectations?
  - o How often do we coach others—1 on 1?
  - o Do we have annual evaluations?

- ☐ Do we discipline to expectations?
  - o Do we have a clear discipline process?
  - o What happens if the performance is not up to standard?
  - o Do we use performance improvement plans to track?

- o Do we have documented training processes and re-training processes to track?
- ☐ Do we reward to expectations?
  - o Do we have a process to reward for good performance?
  - o Are rewards defined?
  - o Are rewards given consistently across company?

Finance Processes:

- ☐ Do we have documented processes for our financial systems?
- ☐ Which ones need to be documented?
- ☐ How do we manage cash flow?
- ☐ What are our payment terms?
- ☐ What are our pricing processes?

Sales & Marketing Processes:

- ☐ What are our sales processes?
- ☐ Do we have a documented sales cycle to follow?
- ☐ Do we use a pipeline for prospect management?
- ☐ Do we have a clear sales incentive plan?
- ☐ Do we have any marketing processes?
- ☐ Do we have an advertising process?
- ☐ What social media processes do we follow?

Departmental Processes:

- ☐ Have we documented the key operational processes per department?
- ☐ Customer service?
- ☐ Manufacturing per product (for tangible businesses)?
- ☐ Types of services delivered (for intangible businesses)?
- ☐ Transportation and delivery (logistics and supply chain)?

Now that you have seen the list of standard business processes, which of these have you written down for your company? You may be surprised how many organizations have **not** written these things down. I've seen many clients with good intentions say they will document processes, but don't follow through. It can be an overwhelming task, but I have some tools that will help you through.

Where is eliminating chaos and confusion on your priority list?

Believe it or not, you need a process to write the process, or this step contributes to the chaos that is already in motion!

One of my business friends, Emily, has a wonderful way of making sure new processes are documented. Her company has a form they refer to as a Standard Operating Procedure (SOP) form. When they need to write a process, they reach for this form.

Emily explains that when they have a customer complaint, the team discusses it by backtracking to uncover the steps that occurred. In many cases, there was no documented process. At that point, the team immediately discusses the best approach to handle the problem. Someone on the team is assigned to write down the agreed-to steps on the SOP form and add it to the SOP manual for future reference. Their SOP form is part of what they define as their *secret sauce*, so I can't share their form with you, but keep reading. I have a format that will work for your business if you don't have one.

Other companies also use forms and templates that they refer to as SOP's (standard operating procedures). It's not an exclusive idea. In Emily's case their SOP, when combined with her other "uniques" in their secret sauce, is what delivers their magic to their customers.

Processes in a checklist format:

If you know your processes, are they on a documented checklist and easy to read?

If you haven't pulled a process out in a while, go find one. I'll wait. You, have it? Here's a checklist of questions about your process checklist:

- ☐ Is it easy to read and understand?
- ☐ If the tasks are followed as written, would the job be done correctly?
- ☐ If not, what is the process to keep processes current?
- ☐ Are all the processes documented in a similar layout and detailed appropriately?

If you do, BRAVO! I'm going to refer to you as Dr. Jekyll.

For those who haven't written the processes down, let's start with creating standard operating procedures forms.

Fig. 5-2 A Standard Operating Procedure (SOP) form to use as your own process-documenting form. It was created following the principles of Dr. Bernice McCarthy about how people learn. Dr. McCarthy created the 4-Mat method which answers the questions: WHAT, WHY, HOW, SO WHAT? *Dr. Bernice McCarthy – About Learning*

Download at: www.LTResults.com/monsterbook/resources

LT Results

Process Name: **Number:**

Who is responsible for this task?
List the position title

What is the brief description of the process?

Why is it important to the company or the job?

When do you do this process? (What happens to tell you it is time to do it?)

How is it done?

☐

☐

☐

☐

☐

☐

☐

☐

☐

Fig. 5-3 An SOP example for a customer-delivery process .

LT Results

	Process Name: Customer Deliveries	**Number:**	D1

Who is responsible for this task? _____ Driver _____
List the position title

What is the brief description of the process?
Deliveries to customer locations

Why is it important to the company or the job?
To fulfill customers' orders and invoices

When do you do this process? (What happens to tell you it is time to do it?)
Each morning at 7 a.m.

How is it done?

☐ Clock in each morning at 6:30 a.m.

☐ Go to truck and follow safety checklist. Note any issues. Sign and take to dispatch.

☐ If truck has issues, immediately contact maintenance to receive estimate on time to repair.

☐ Report at 7 a.m. to dispatch

☐ Dispatch distributes list of delivery cards to drivers for the day with expected delivery times.

☐ Take delivery cards to warehouse team.

☐ Together we load deliveries as per expected offload delivery times.

☐ Check each loaded delivery against warehouse master log for day.

☐ When all loaded, warehouse and driver both sign warehouse master log with time completed.

In this example, you could break the above down further to create two processes. One for truck safety procedures and one for customer deliveries.

One or Two Processes?

How do you know if it should be one, two, or more processes? If you find it hard to define or feel overwhelmed thinking about the steps, that is a clue that you are trying to document too big of a task. Think about the task or concept and break it down into simpler processes to document. Always keep in mind, the tasks should be relatively short and easy to understand. The test of a good process checklist is to hand the checklist to someone new and ask them if they can understand the steps and perform them. This process can then become a training tool as well. Yahoo! Multiple uses!

There are many books on the market that talk about processes. My favorites are *Traction* by Gino Wickman, *Scaling Up* by Verne Harnish, and *Navigating the Growth Curve* by James Fischer. Documenting process does not have to be hard. Make a simple checklist with simple language so that *anyone* can help you write them down. Get the process down once, then you can go back and refine as necessary.

Once Written, Where Does It Go?

I recommend two places for your process documentation. 1) Keep each checklist on a shared drive in your company computer system where it can be updated and referenced by anyone who needs the information. 2) Keep a printed version in a binder near the task or workstation for easy reference.

Use for Training:

I mentioned earlier, a third way to use these processes is for training new hires or employees new to this job. You can video record your checklists or SOPs. I use LOOM to train my assistants, but Zoom, Slack, Google Drive, or just your phone camera could work. Use the application you're comfortable with.

The reason I like this method is that at any time of day or night, I can sit at my computer, pull up a particular application or form I need someone to learn, then videotape myself carrying out that process. I talk through it and demonstrate the steps as I show the documents or application on my desktop computer. I explain: 1) *what* needs to be done, 2) *why* it needs to be done, 3) *how* it needs to be done, 4) if not done *what could happen*. Just like the SOP format I shared.

Then I add the new video to my video bank of process checklists to become a standard operating procedures digital file for my company. It also becomes my training curriculum to orient new employees, to cross-train, or to retrain, in the case of a poor performer. I recommend you try this method; I think you'll find it to be a quick and easy way to document your own processes.

Okay, I hear you. You don't have time to do this, and you need help. If you had the processes down it would be easy to hire and get someone in, but you're so busy you can't stop to even think or eat, let alone to videotape and write checklists.

For those of you in that situation (and there are many of you), there are a few ways to tackle this. I've used the following techniques with some of my clients and urge you to use one or two.

For existing staff with no written processes.

1. Get with your team members and jointly brainstorm the key processes of the company.
2. Prioritize the list if you can.

3. Assign the processes out and set a deadline.

4. Schedule a check-in time halfway through to ensure everyone is on schedule.

5. Hold the staff accountable for completing the process.

Other ideas for how to get your processes written:

- **Interview style:**

    o Hire someone to interview the job holder. Have the interviewer write out the processes as the job holder speaks or does the process. The interviewer types up the steps and sends it to the job holder and leader to review and make edits. Voilà! You've got a task documented.

    o I strive to look for ways to save money for clients. This is a perfect task for an intern, a student looking for a summer job, or spouse looking to learn more about the company. It also allows the family to contribute to the organization in a meaningful way.

- **At one of your regular meetings or a special off-site meeting:**

    o Assign your team members the processes for their job and request they write them up in a checklist format. (As per a sample). Set the timer for an hour.

    o Assign teams of two—ask one person to interview the other about the key processes they do in their job. The person who interviews also documents, and then vice-versa. This way, you cross-train the pair as well.

- **With some fun:**
  - o Turn on a video camera or phone camera. Ask one employee to play a new employee while the process owner describes how the job is done. Voilà, you have a training program with the key company processes videotaped. The staff can have some fun with the videotape, as long as the steps are clear. You could make it a competition for best drama.
  - o Make updating existing processes an agenda item for an annual meeting.

- **If orienting a new employee and the process steps are not written down:**
  - o You may have to train verbally and demonstrate for a new employee what needs to be done. If so, ask them to take notes and type up what they heard you say in a checklist format.
  - o If you have time, do a Loom video after hours to give the new employee instructions. Ask the new employee to watch the video during the day and document the checklist that you described. You can then quickly correct and edit the document, and have it become one of the official processes for that job.

Processes are a big area to tackle, but once they are done your organization will run more smoothly, and the #1 chaos-creator will be managed.

Other Chaos-Creators:

There are other things that can become chaos-creators. If you do not accomplish some of the actions from the earlier chapters, i.e., vision, values, etc., they will show up eventually and create chaos. This is not a full list, but these are the ones to pay attention to first. Reflect on your workplace and note which seem to be occurring.

☐ **Lack of focus:** Are you following your strategic vision? Or just going after *any shiny object* that can make money? You will find the more narrowly you focus your business, the more opportunities that show up in that arena. Does the team know the company goals and objectives? Have you communicated them? If not, it will be impossible to achieve those goals and objectives. What is the direction for the year, quarter, month, or week? What is the company trying to accomplish?

☐ **Overcontrol:** By you or one of your leaders? This can result from fear. But what's behind the fear? Is it that:

    o   You don't know what to do next and don't trust your team to know? Is that because you don't have a strategic focus to align your plans around, or is there some other reason?

    o   People don't know what to do next? Is the priority of the work unclear, or processes undocumented so you must guide people through every step or task.

o No one does what's asked? Do you micromanage every employee task? Are your roles and responsibilities clear? Do people know their jobs? Do you hold performance conversations with staff and help them see what they are doing well and what needs to improve?

o There's not enough staff to do the work? You have no choice but to do it yourself?

o No one stays around once you've trained them, and you must step back in? Have you stopped to ask why they are leaving? Do you let go and let them do their job once they are trained?

o You believe that employees cannot think for themselves? You search for examples to prove your belief? Your belief becomes a behavioral action. Change your belief and your employees' behavior will change.

o You don't know how to let go? To overcome the overcontrol, ask for people's help according to their strengths, and trust them to do their job.

☐ **Under control:** By you or one of your leaders. This can also be because of fear. Potential reasons:

o You fear that you don't know what to do next? You need to work to align your strategic vision with objectives and goals.

- o You or your team are so overwhelmed with trying to capture every opportunity that your team is confused and doesn't know what to do next?

- o Because of confusion and lack of direction, employees are doing whatever is easiest or the first thing they see to be done?

- o You fear that you don't have time? Others are left on their own and you expect them to figure it out, as your belief is, *that's what you pay them to do*? That attitude won't get you very far. You must work smarter to enable others to do the job. You can assign others to cross-train, or you must slow down the customer orders long enough to train your staff in their roles.

- ☐ **Lack of support:**

  - o You don't have anyone to delegate to.

    - ■ Is it because you are afraid to hire? Take a leap of faith and hire.

    - ■ Do you have enough cash allotted? Do you know how much this person's salary will cost? Define how this position will pay for itself. If it is not a revenue-producing position, define how the position helps others be more productive.

    - ■ Can you contract out tasks that are not your strengths? Accounting services, office administration to help with your calendar and emails, web services, fractional sales, or fractional chief financial officer? Don't overlook virtual assistants.

- o You have someone to delegate to, but you are not delegating.

  - ■ Is this from overcontrol, lack of trust, or not taking the time to teach and delegate. Let's turn this business around and begin to take that step of courage to trust and delegate some of your tasks and free your time to spend elsewhere. Your role is to lead the organization.

  - ■ Do you know your people? What strengths do they have? If not sure, ask for volunteers for tasks that need to be delegated. Normally people who have those skill areas want to do more in their areas of strength and will be excited to assist.

Delegating works well when done correctly. Following a set of steps will ensure the project or job is completed as expected.

Fig. 5-4, Steps to Delegate

Steps to Delegate:

- Describe the end result being desired.
- Tell the person what you need them to do specifically. Show the checklist or explain the task. Ensuring they are taking notes.
- Do the task/process in front of them as they observe the checklist or write the steps down.
- Ask them to now do the process in front of you using the checklist or their notes and restate their understanding of the end result.
- Determine how comfortable you both feel with the process and ask the employee if they have any questions or other ideas to accomplish the task. (If they have ideas you want to hear them now to decide if the process could be improved. You do not want them making changes arbitrarily).
- Agree on a time to check back with them to see how they are doing. Make sure you are both comfortable with the time frame, otherwise adjust it.
- Meet at the agreed time. Review what's going well, what's not, and where they got stuck.
- If there is no written process for this task –make sure they have taken notes and you can now review the completed document throughout to approve it.

If you become aware of these areas, you will eliminate many of the chaos-creators.

Here's how Dr. Jekyll, our logical and organized scientist, would start.

- He would focus on his company's purpose and the direction he wants to go using his vision and a strategic plan (as we discussed in Chapter 2). He would make sure the actions he takes are underpinned by the strategy. He would communicate to the team weekly, monthly, quarterly, etc.

- He would make his decisions based on his values, and everyone in the team would know the criteria he uses for decision-making.

- He would have a clear organizational structure and clear roles and responsibilities documented for each team member so they understand where they fit in the chain of command.

- The core company processes would be documented and available in multiple formats and locations to ensure everyone knows who, where, when, and how the processes are done.

- He would verify that people's tasks are clear and delegate to those who would best fit the task or ask for volunteers.

- He would be patient and take the steps necessary to delegate the job. But if he were swamped with work, he would make a video to explain what he needs and send it to that person to get the person started. He would then check back to make sure they understand.

- These actions would eliminate chaos in Dr. Jekyll's business.

Here is a reminder from earlier in the chapter of some to-do's to remember:

Your Actions:

- Define your secret sauce. Work with your team to define what you do differently from the competition that makes you unique.

- Have the team write out the secret sauce process steps to make this repeatable (also referred to as scaleable) and part of your business identity.

 **Moment to Change**

As you consider the chaos-creators from this chapter,

Are you more like Dr. Jekyll? 	Are you more like Mr. Hyde? 

Whichever you are, there are things you can each do to continually improve.

1. What can you start doing to eliminate the chaos?

2. What can you stop doing to eliminate the chaos?

3. What can you continue doing to eliminate the chaos?

"All great changes are preceded by chaos."
—Deepak Chopra

Now, your conversation with your spouse or partner sounds like this:

> **"Don't you need to check in with anyone at the plant before we go?"**
> **You say, "No, it is under control. Let's go."**

---

* Footnote: Dr. Bernice McCarthy (USA) developed the first basic structure of the 4MAT system in the late 1970s. Since then, the method has systematically and continuously been used, developed and linked to the newest research in the field.

Chapter 6

Emotional Outbursts: Keep Stress & Emotions in Check

Welcome back, Leader! We've delved deep into your business at this point, and I hope you feel like we're friends by now, because we're about to get into a potentially sensitive topic. In the last chapter we discussed what creates chaos. Were you able to put your finger on the chaos-creator that affects your business most significantly? Now we get into the drama that occurs because of that chaos. I am speaking about unchecked emotions. This is when Mr. Hyde's menacing and sometimes monster-like behaviors show up at work and at home.

A spouse or partner says:

> *"It's like you are two people—one moment nice as pie, the second, a monster!*
> *You're either withdrawn and silent, or you are angry and screaming at us!"*

STRESS! It is the precursor to emotional drama that can occur in your work environments.

An example of stress in the workplace might be something like this: You receive a big order at a time when cash flow is critically low. You need the money as soon as possible, so you promise your customer a quick turnaround. However, materials for assembly arrive late. Pressure on you steadily builds as you push your team to meet the short deadline and deliver to your customer as promised. Phew! It's done!

You can see from this one example how stress can build in workplace situations. You must realize how this buildup of stress can affect leadership. Besides mental and emotional symptoms, stress actually causes our body to physically react and build up *more* tension via a hormone called cortisol. Cortisol is a steroid hormone that your adrenal glands produce, and *you have no control over its production.* High cortisol levels must be reduced to relieve stress. If not, at some point you will blow up like a pressure cooker unable to release steam.

Stress is unavoidable in our world. Stress in small amounts can actually be motivating and productive, but excessive stress is crippling, and you may not even recognize its presence.

How do you know if you're experiencing workplace stress?

You may find instances in which you have lost your confidence and feel like an imposter in your position. You may feel like everything is out of your control. Maybe you've lost one of your managers or supervisors and now must assume additional roles and responsibilities again. You may be angry, irritable, or withdrawn. Other symptoms include anxiety, apathy, disinterest in work, insomnia, fatigue, difficulty concentrating, headaches, muscle tension, digestion issues, social withdrawal, or use of drugs or alcohol to cope.

Stress can be addressed **before** it erupts into emotional outbursts or toxic behavior. Any job can have stressful elements, even if you love what you do. Some stress at work is normal, however excessive stress will obstruct your productivity and impact your physical and emotional health if left unchecked.

There are situations you can't control in your work environment, but that doesn't mean you're powerless—even when you're stuck in a problematic situation. Managing stress isn't about making huge changes or rethinking career ambitions, but rather about focusing on the things within your control.

Stress at work can be defined as, "the harmful physical and emotional responses that occur when the requirements of the job do not match the capabilities, resources, or needs of the worker." Stress at work can lead to poor health, frequent sick days, and injury. A healthy work environment is one where the pressures on employees are relevant to their abilities and resources, to the amount of control they have over their work, and to the support they receive.

By taking a deeper look at types of stress, sources of stress, and levels of stress within your organization, you can create meaningful change that guards against the inevitable outcomes of unabated stress.

The following are statistics from a Zippia Research article, "40+ Worrisome Workplace Stress Statistics [2022]: Facts, Causes, and Trends," by Caitlin Mazur, January 23, 2022, provides a context to what is occurring within organizations around stress.

Fig. 6-1, Causes of Workplace Stress

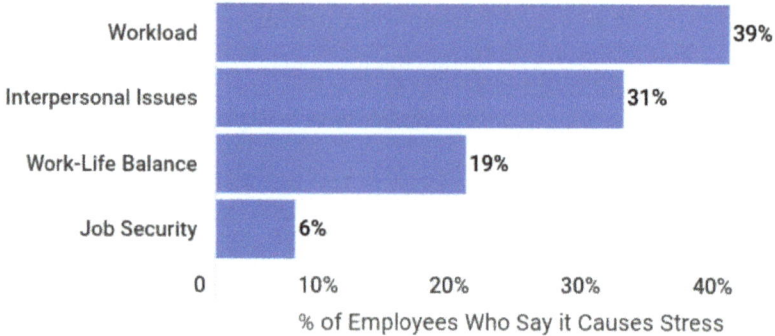

The alarming statistics around workplace stress only continue to grow, pointing to much-needed change in expectations, mental health resources, and work-life balance. Through our research, (research references all dated 2021), we found:

- 55% of Americans are stressed during the day.

- Some 57% of U.S. and Canadian workers reported feeling stress on a daily basis, compared with 43% of people who feel that way globally. Americans and Canadians' rate of daily job-related stress is also up 8% year-over-year.

- Only 6% of workers report not feeling stressed at work. Around 23% of workers described their stress levels as high, while 6% said their stress levels were unreasonably high.

- 30% of survey respondents stated that their job or careers were regular causes of stress. Among Millennials and Gen Z, this statistic jumps to 44%, showing that stress is on the rise among younger generations and presents a larger global problem than it did 20 or 30 years ago.

• 48% of employees agreed they felt more callous toward people since they took their job.

• 65% of workers said that workplace stress had caused difficulties, and more than 10% described these as having major effects on their life.

• 42% of employees report that yelling and other verbal abuse is common, while 29% have yelled at co-workers because of workplace stress.

• *On a scale from one to ten, the average American rates their stress level as 4.9.*

These are shocking statistics! I recommend you understand your own stress levels and those of your team members. Stress assessments that accurately gauge these are available. My business uses a high-quality online stress assessment called the Stress Quotient, created by Target Training International (TTI). Chapter 10 contains additional information about this tool. Alternately, learn the factors that create stress and watch for stress symptoms among your team.

Here is a one-page snapshot from TTI's stress quotient to help you focus on specific areas of stress.

Fig. 6-2 , TTI Stress Quotient - Stress Symptoms Index

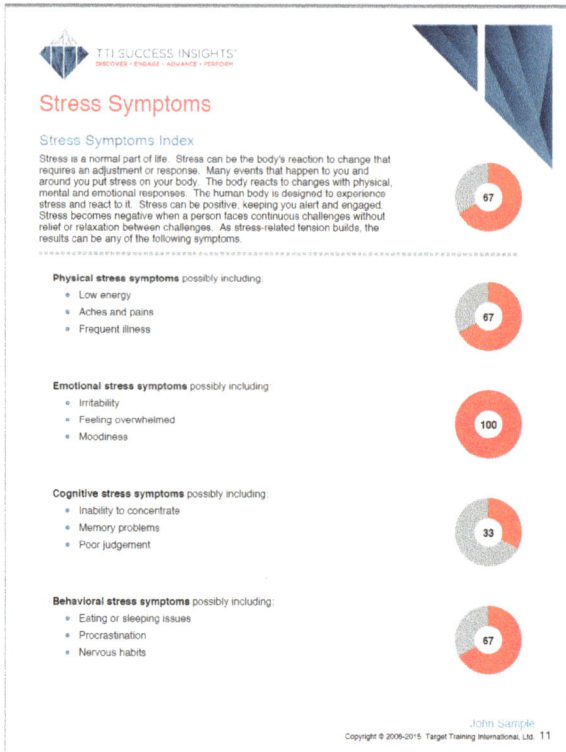

Encourage your employees to release their stress in healthy ways to prevent emotional explosions in the workplace. Try these tips, based on recommendations from The Mayo Clinic https://www.mayoclinic.org/healthy-lifestyle/stress-management/in-depth/stress-relievers/art-20047257:

1. Get active. Any form of physical activity can act as a stress reliever.

2. Eat a healthy diet.

3. Avoid unhealthy habits.

4. Meditate.

5. Laugh more.

6. Connect with others.

7. Assert yourself.

8. Try yoga.

9. Get enough sleep.

10. Keep a journal.

11. Get musical and creative.

12. Seek counseling.

This is a good self-check for you, as business leaders, too. Self-care is our responsibility and is guaranteed to make you a stronger, better leader with more clarity—and be a good example for staff.

I'd like to highlight one statistic from the research above that specifically deals with our chapter topic:

"42% of employees report that yelling and other verbal abuse is common, while 29% have yelled at co-workers because of workplace stress."

Unfortunately, these behaviors show up everywhere, not just in owners and leaders, but in individuals who deal with chaos personally or professionally. Where there is pressure, confusion, or uncertainty, fear shows up. When fear shows up, an individual's personal needs will not be met. The person in such circumstances may withdraw, have an emotional outburst, display erratic behavior, or worse.

This chart provides examples and definitions of various behaviors that can be stress-induced; the chart that follows references other underlying emotional behaviors as well. If you are close to these behaviors on a regular basis, you may think they are normal and that everyone has them. Be advised, **these are not normal**. (These are based on descriptions from www.mayoclinic.org.)

Fig. 6-3, Types of Emotional Behaviors

Emotional Outburst	Erratic Behavior	Toxic Behavior
	Lack of consistency, regularity, or uniformity. Deviating from what is ordinary and standard.	Extremely harsh, malicious, or harmful. Not all descriptions are stress-induced and may reference
• Sudden irritability • Fits of crying or laughter • Feeling angry, but not knowing why • Angry outbursts • Strong or exaggerated feelings of any kind	• Unpredictable, irregular, and no stable outcome • Actions that often blindside those around them • Aggressiveness • Temper tantrums • Tirades • Heated arguments • Shouting • Slapping, shoving or pushing • Physical fights • Property damage • Threatening or assaulting people or animals	• Difficulty regulating emotions and behaviors • Cynical, sullen, or hostile attitude • Significant interpersonal problems • No respect for others' boundaries • Exaggerated sense of self-importance and entitlement • Resentment and opposition of the demands of others, especially people in authority • Intense anxiety and panic attacks • Taking advantage of others to get what they want • Monopolizing conversations and belittling others • Abuse of alcohol and other substances

Descriptions originated from www.mayoclinic.org

If you observe any of these behaviors, address them quickly to keep your organization healthy, productive, and safe. You may have an occasional outburst over stress, but it is more concerning if you repeat the behavior. Be alert to these behaviors in your workplace.

What if it's you, the leader, behaving in this way?

How aware are you of your own behavior? Has your spouse ever suggested that you have erratic behavior, as per our quote example at the beginning of the chapter? Have you ever assessed yourself to check your own emotional awareness?

Before I recommend a psychologist (though I think anyone could benefit from time with a professional), I want to remind you that sometimes you bring on your emotional behavior yourself. In some cases, you may have a **belief** about what others in society expect you to be. Beliefs such as:

- We must be all things to all people.

- We can never say no.

- We must hide how we really feel because others' feelings are more important.

- Men shouldn't cry as it exposes vulnerabilities.

- If women cry, they look like they can't handle the job.

What's real and true for you? Spend some time reflecting on these belief statements. I suggest you ask a trusted friend or partner to be honest with you about their experience with your interactions.

When a societal belief collides with your own personal beliefs about who you are or who you want to be, you will be out of personal alignment. I mentioned in Chapter 3 the importance of getting clear with your beliefs first, then aligning to your values. If you do not do this, the resulting disconnect in your mind and heart can result in physical distress in your body. The disconnect can cause emotional, erratic, and toxic behaviors in the workplace or at home. If your behaviors are erratic or toxic, please seek a professional to help you work through your emotions.

How to personally deal with toxic behavior if you see it:

- Stay calm.

- Don't take what is said personally.

- Be aware of the timing of what you say; read the room.

- Don't let your own ego get out of control.

- Look for triggers or patterns.

- Respectfully tell the individual, even if it is your boss, when their words are offensive, not appreciated, or inappropriate.

- If you are fearful of talking to your boss, go to another leader or HR regarding your manager's communication or behaviors and explain how they impact your work.

- Model the behavior you expect from others, including your boss.

- Offer to deliver training on workplace communication.

- Go somewhere you feel safe.

- Know when to get outside help.

- Know when it is time to leave the company.

If the toxic behavior occurs in a team setting, here are three ways to address it:

- Create a strong sense of team cohesion. A group setting makes dysfunctional acting out more noticeable, more controllable, more discussable, and therefore less acceptable. Peer pressure will push those with toxic behavior to adapt to the group's norms. Thus, it is the peers who will take on the role of "enforcers," to encourage the disrupters to listen and empathize with others.

- Use this strong team to promote peer feedback. For those with toxic behavior, it's often less threatening to receive feedback from peers, rather than from a single person or leader. Feedback from many people is harder to ignore than feedback from one person. If the dynamics of the group are facilitated effectively, the disrupter's view of themselves will be revealed, mirrored, and challenged, and can be modified.

- Create a safe, somewhat playful space. This can become an environment where people with a poor disposition learn to develop trust, explore boundaries, accept feedback, and increase self-awareness. In such a setting, the disrupter's peers will be able to constructively confront problematic behavior while simultaneously offering a modicum of understanding.

In every situation, you have a choice, even when it doesn't feel as if you do. An outside perspective may be necessary, so don't be afraid to ask for help.

An example in the workplace

I once worked for a Mr. Hyde boss. I'd like to share the story, then pull the lessons from my example.

I worked in a sales department in a large city. Every Friday the sales team had one-on-one discussions with the boss regarding that week's performance and plans for the upcoming one. The meetings were scheduled based on seniority. The longer-term representatives had the morning timeslots, and the less senior employees were later. Since I was the newest, my time slot was 5:00 every Friday afternoon. Inevitably, every Friday others ran long, and as a result my meeting finished at 6:30 or 7:00. By that time, the entire sales team was next door having drinks while I was still at my one-on-one in the office.

My boss was a very nice individual that I liked very much—until they became stressed. When under stress, my boss became very tense and agitated. I saw them display erratic behavior, especially on Fridays. I never knew if they would berate me or compliment me.

It was a regular practice for salespeople, before we entered the office Monday through Friday, to first call reception and find out if the boss was in that day. If yes, we asked for a mood check. Depending on that answer, we determined how badly we needed to be in the office to complete our work. If the boss was in, and in a bad mood, I'd always figure out another way to do my work without being there.

Fridays were especially bad because of the meeting schedule. The boss could start out with a very fun-loving, jovial attitude, but by the time I had my 5:00 (usually at 6:00) they were tired and irritable. I had to be hypervigilant as I managed the potential minefield of my boss's questions. Often, I gave an answer that I thought they wanted to hear, rather than take the brunt of their emotions with the real answer.

How many of you have been in this situation? As much as you wanted to be a strong performer, it was difficult if you had a Mr. Hyde boss. Unfortunately, I'm not sure that my boss knew they were perceived negatively by others or had ever gotten constructive feedback.

The lessons?

We forget there are multiple perspectives to a story, and only look at the one that impacts us, without stopping to put ourselves in the other's shoes. Though the Mr. Hyde's behaviors were erratic and bordered on toxic, had anyone ever addressed that with them and held them accountable to change? Was someone else in the office demonstrating disruptive behavior with my boss before my meeting?

As I reflect on this experience, I now realize the Friday afternoon mood change could have been because my boss, Mr. Hyde, missed being with their family every Friday evening, and never had an early out on Fridays because of these late running meetings. Back then, it was about me not being able to meet my friends in the bar after work, but now I realize Mr. Hyde couldn't get out and enjoy their Friday evening either.

Being able to see patterns of behavior will help you help someone else, even if you are not their boss. Don't forget to stop and see things from the other person's perspective. You might ask yourself:

- Is there a pattern to the behavior? Every day? Or only when under stress?
- Do certain people set off Mr. Hyde?
- Are there certain locations or times of day when this occurs?
- What about the situation could set off Mr. Hyde if you look at it from their perspective?

You've observed the disruptive behavior, now what? Take it to your manager or HR person for help. If the behavior is from your direct-line manager, find another leader for assistance, if you have no HR and don't feel comfortable addressing them on your own.

What if it's YOU?

What if you are the Mr. Hyde? This is a moment of choice. Do you want to change? Do you want to stop the behavior? I hope you will spend time working on yourself with the tools that follow and those in Chapter 10. I encourage every leader to get a coach, just as highly paid athletes do. It gives you a sounding board. In some cases, you may want to work with a therapist for professional assistance.

Consequences of our Behavioral Actions

Let's build two more steps onto the chart we used in Chapter 3.

Fig. 6-4 Triggered Beliefs & Values Drive Behaviors with Consequences

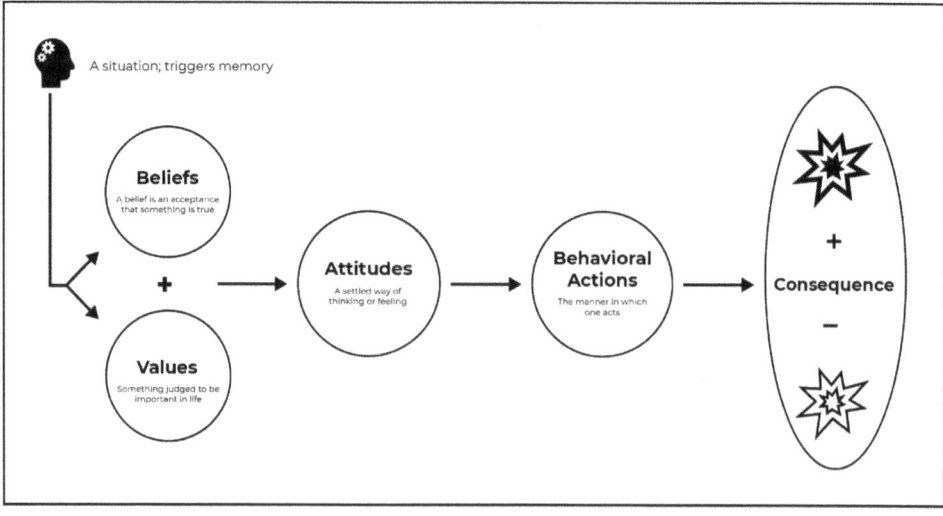

Let's use the experience I had with my boss to walk through this model and its two new steps. I hear that Mr. Hyde is in a bad mood or angry. That triggers me (an event or situation reminds me) to think of my father and the experiences I had when he was angry. The belief I had was that my father was never wrong, so I must be wrong and in trouble. Similarly, if I meet with Mr. Hyde and he's upset, I'm feeling that I will be found to have done something wrong, just like I remember with my father. Even if I knew I hadn't done anything wrong, I was fearful of being wrong and humiliated or embarrassed. My attitude was fear. My behavioral actions were to stay away from Mr. Hyde and the office when he was angry or in a bad mood.

Our behavior results in positive or negative consequences for us. It is important to realize if the consequence to the triggered behavior was what I intended to receive for myself? In my case, I had both a positive and a negative consequence.

The positive consequence was that by avoiding Mr. Hyde, I was free of the fear of getting in trouble. The negative consequence was that I lacked information I needed to get from the office, and because I did not have it, my sale was delayed, and I did not deliver as promised to my customer and did not hold true to my word (violation of my personal values). Was that the consequence I wanted? No, I did not want to wait on the sale and be unable to follow up appropriately. The impact of my beliefs had made me tell myself a story—that I was in trouble—instead of simply going to the office for the material I needed to close the sale on time and as promised to my customer. To change that outcome in the future, I have to go back to my core beliefs and values and re-program myself to understand what is true and real in my beliefs, not imagined.

You can see the impact behaviors can have on us and others from my one example. My experience happened 38 years ago, and I still remember it vividly. Make sure you are not leaving any trigger-trails in your interactions.

How to deal with Emotional Behavior

As leaders, we must develop skills to deal with emotional behaviors that erupt on the job, especially in today's workplace. Before you can do that effectively, you must first consider how emotional outbursts trigger you. What beliefs and attitudes run through your head when an emotional outburst occurs? How will you cope with your reactions and respond most constructively? Remember, there will be positive or negative consequences from the actions you take in that moment. Plan and discuss potential scenarios with a mentor or coach. Let them help you think through situations and practice your actions to ensure you are not emotionally charged and reacting to triggers in that moment.

My husband is a retired flight mechanic who ran the search-and-rescue basket for helicopter missions with the U.S. Coast Guard. He and the crew constantly trained and cross-trained during their down time. The reason they did this was to ensure that when emotionally charged situations occurred, no one panicked. Their training overrode any kind of emotional response. A good leader will make that their mission, too.

Key Actions to Deal with Emotional Behavior

Learn these key actions (from Zenger-Miller Frontline Leadership program), and you will be ready to manage whatever emotional behavior comes your way.

Fig. 6-5 The Key Actions for Emotional Behavior,

www.LTResults.com/monsterbook/resources

The Key Actions for Emotional Behavior are:

1. Calmly acknowledge the emotional behavior.
2. Describe the impact the emotional behavior is having on you and on the discussion.
3. Determine if it's possible to continue the discussion constructively.
4. Propose an approach for jointly re-focusing on the work issue.
5. Express support and reassurance.

Copyright © 1986 by Zenger-Miller

---

1. **Calmly acknowledge the emotional behavior.** (Use the phrase, "You look…(emotion)". If not sure, use, "You look (mad), (sad), or (glad), they will correct you with the proper emotion.)

2. **Describe the impact the emotional behavior is having on you and on the discussion.** (It upsets me when you're (emotion) as I can't keep my focus on the discussion in the team meeting.)

3. **Determine if it's possible to continue the discussion constructively.** (Are we able to continue this conversation now or do you need some to collect yourself?)

4. **Propose an approach for jointly re-focusing on the work issue.** (In the future, what if, when this topic comes up…)

Unless you work alone, you will witness emotional behavior in your workplace. Learn how to address it. It will make you a stronger leader.

"CEOs are hired for their intellect and business expertise – and fired for a lack of emotional intelligence."
— Daniel Goleman

Emotional Intelligence

Emotional Intelligence (EQ or EI) is important to develop in the world today. We all need to increase our self-awareness and social awareness. EQ is a measure of our emotional intelligence. It indicates how well we manage our emotions and impact our relationships with others. This measurement ties to seven basic emotions: joy, surprise, sadness, fear, contempt, anger, and disgust.

While the term "emotional intelligence" was first defined in 1990 by psychologists John D. Mayer and Peter Salovey, it took the ground-breaking book by Daniel Goleman (*Emotional Intelligence*, 1995), to bring it to the forefront of business. Goleman asserted that **90% of the difference between star performers and average performers in the workplace was related to emotional intelligence (EQ).** The role of emotions in conflict resolution, collaboration, innovation, and other key successful cultural attributes in companies is also well documented.

Research shows that developing greater emotional intelligence can lead to higher performance and compensation, as well as better professional and personal relationships. Which means, the better you understand and manage your emotions—and the emotions of people around you—the greater your chances of success!

Take a look at these statistics:

> *1. 95% of people think they are self-aware, but only 10–15% actually are.*
>
> *(Harvard Business Review)*
>
> *2. 90% of top-performing employees have high emotional intelligence.*
>
> *(Center for Innovative Public Health Research)*
>
> *3. 75% of the Fortune 500 companies use emotional intelligence training tools.*
>
> *(Vantage Circle)*
>
> *4. EQ is four times more effective than IQ in determining who will be successful in their field. (LinkedIn)*
>
> *A 40-year study of UC Berkeley PhDs showed that EQ is four times more powerful than IQ in determining a person's success in their given field. Skills like active listening, stress management, and empathy are contributing factors to a person's success.*
>
> *5. Leaders with empathy perform over 40% higher in employee engagement, decision-making, and coaching. (Harvard Business School)*
>
> *Empathy is the number one skill that leaders must be good at. Research shows that managers or employees in a leadership role are perceived to have better job performance when they are empathetic. When leaders communicate to their direct reports with empathy, the team feels more supported, and individual members perform better.*
>
> *6. 44 Fortune 500 companies found that salespeople with high EQ brought in twice as much revenue as those with low to average emotional intelligence.*
>
> *(International Risk Management Institute)*

As we know, there is more to business than the bottom line. To keep employees engaged and productivity high, employers must look at the additional benefits of the work environment. Can my employees work together well despite competing priorities and ideas? Can my employees show more compassion towards each other, customers, and partners to resolve never-ending business challenges? Do my employees feel valued? Do we have a culture that nurtures happiness or positivity? How can I maximize the potential of my workforce? The answers to these questions are not always solved by a higher paycheck.

Daniel Goleman categorized emotional intelligence into five domains. They are:

Emotional Intelligence—Self: What goes on inside of you as you experience day-to-day events.

- Self-Awareness is being aware of how your actions and emotions can affect those around you.

- Self-Regulation is about keeping yourself in check, so you don't make rushed decisions or compromise your code of ethics.

- Motivation is a passion to work for reasons that go beyond the external drive for knowledge, utility, sur-roundings, others, power, or methodology. It is based on an internal drive or propensity to pursue goals with energy and persistence.

Emotional Intelligence—Others: What goes on between you and others.

- Social Awareness is the ability to understand the emotional makeup of other people and how your words and actions affect others. (Empathy)
- Social Regulation is your ability to influence the emotional clarity of others by managing relationships and building networks. (Social Skills)

How can we use this information?

Learn about it, read about it, and self-assess. Practice paying attention to social cues. Think before you speak. Watch how others react. Work to build relationships and personal or business networks.

TTI Success Insights provides an online **Emotional Quotient** assessment based on Daniel Goleman's breakdown of the domains. The reports identify areas of growth and strengths in one's emotional intelligence. If you'd like access to the tool, go to Chapter 10 for more details.

Two of the customized report pages follow to show you what such a report illustrates.

Fig. 6-6, TTI Emotional Quotient Dimensions™ and 6-7, TTI Emotional Quotient™ Wheel

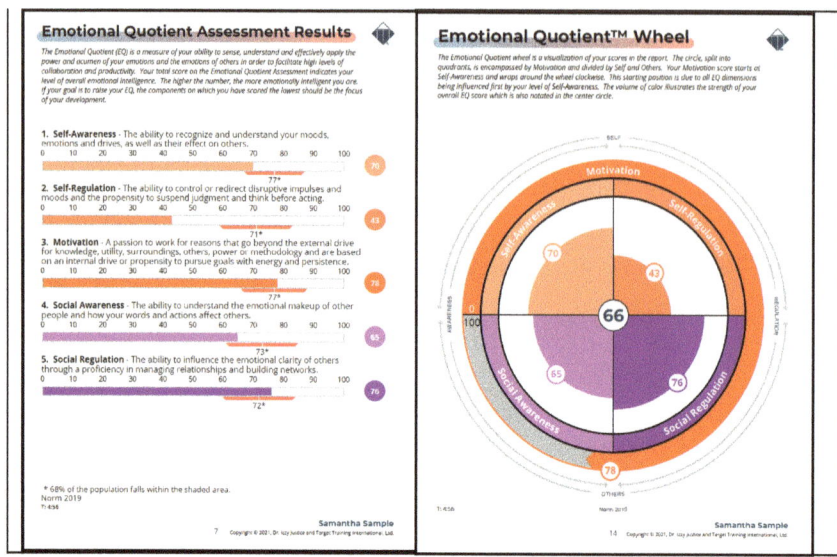

Emotional competence is essential in environments that require people to deal with constantly changing emotional temperatures of people, situations, and roles, as well as pressure to innovate. Due to the pandemic, we now have people who work from home, share positions, or move from project to project. Consequently, the ability to manage relationships has become even more critical today.

What can you do until you have time to self-assess? Refer to these tips from https://positivepsychology.com/emotional-intelligence-exercises

Tips for Enhancing Your Own Emotional Intelligence

1. *Reflect on your own emotions.*

2. *Ask others for perspective.*

3. *Be observant (of your own emotions).*

4. *Use "the pause" (e.g., taking a moment to think before speaking).*

5. *Explore the "why" (bridge the gap by taking someone else's perspective).*

6. *When criticized, don't take offense. Instead, ask: What can I learn?*

7. *Practice, practice, practice (Bariso, 2016) .*

If you're looking to enhance your team's emotional intelligence, keep these 7 tips in mind:

Tips for Enhancing the Emotional Intelligence of Teams

1. *Have a ringleader.*

2. *Identify team members' strengths and weaknesses.*

3. *Spark passion.*

4. *Build team norms.*

5. *Develop creative ways to manage stress.*

6. *Allow team members to have a voice.*

7. *Encourage employees to work and play together (Rampton, n.d.) .*

 **Moment to Change**

Are you more like Dr. Jekyll?	Are you more like Mr. Hyde?
You exhibit few emotional outbursts, no erratic behavior, and no toxic behavior. You behave kindly.	You exhibit a number of emotional outbursts, erratic behavior, and /or toxic behavior with varying degrees of intensity. You can be unpredictable and disruptive.

There is room for growth whichever style you have. It's all about self-awareness and respect for others.

1. What can you start doing?

2. What can you stop doing?

3. There are many things you are doing correctly. What can you continue to do to keep the environment free of disruptive behaviors?

Your spouse now says,

> *"Oh Sweetheart, that is so thoughtful and considerate of you. You planned all of this for us?"*

Next chapter, we look at cash. Cash can make many of us emotional!

Cash Flow Crunch!
Get On Top of Cash Flow

Dear Leader, I hope the last chapter helped you look at yourself and identify your emotional blind spots. If you've had difficulty, remember sometimes it is easier to get feedback from an objective third party. I also encourage you to work through any behavioral issues you exhibit so you can become the Dr. Jekyll leader your people respect.

It is a good thing emotions are in check because your spouse or partner says…

> *"Where's the money? We're always waiting for the next check."*

Money! It can seem like a monster that brings all kinds of issues and beliefs to the surface, no matter how long you've been in business. At one time or another most businesses deal with cash flow issues, such as not enough to make payroll, too much tied up in inventory, low sales, or slow paying customers. When any of these occur, in that moment nothing is more important than getting the cash flowing. Cash flow problems can happen at any time in your business evolution—just starting out, after you hire new employees, or ten years down the road when a sudden economic downturn affects your business. Any time cash flow problems occur, they are likely accompanied by strong emotions. Please note that I purposely discuss this *after* the chapter on emotions so you can be more aware of any lingering emotional behavior first!

Poor cash flow affects individuals differently. I will address 1) how it impacts the leader, both personally and professionally, 2) how it impacts the team, and 3) solutions to resolve cash flow issues and move forward.

The easiest way to address these topics is to tell you my personal cash flow story and pull the lessons out. I have no doubt that my story will make you feel a whole lot better about your situation! I mentioned earlier that I have owned my consulting business for 23 years. You might think I'd have learned my cash flow lessons more quickly, but it took many repeated lessons over those 23 years to change my financial behavior. I honestly didn't realize how many lessons I'd had until I wrote this chapter! Eeeegads! Where was my self-awareness?!

In 2000 my business was two years old, and it was tough. I was a single mom living with my son in Hong Kong; cost of living was very high. I needed more income than my sole client could provide, so I quickly aligned with a consulting group and made additional revenue to get back on track. In Hong Kong, if you didn't financially right yourself quickly, you'd be selling everything you owned. (And yes, I had that experience, too.)

In those early years I had the best intentions to keep my business finances separate from my personal ones. But I found that by the time the checks arrived, I needed immediate funds to pay for groceries and bills. I would use the business money rather than make a transfer to my personal account. Whatever priority was hottest that day was where the cash went.

I'd like to bring forward a point in the part of my story that follows. That point is that our business finances affect others, too. In my case, it was my son. Before I became a sole entrepreneur, I was an international employee of DHL. As such I received some pretty nice perks, including a travel stipend. If I was shrewd with my travel money, I could make some home visits to the U.S., *and* take some vacation trips, too. Between the ages of two and eight, my son, Cole and I, took some pretty cool trips—like "down under" to Australia, on an African safari, and a walk on the Great Wall of China. I loved being able to make exotic lifelong memories with him.

When Cole was ten, I had started my own business and my personal finances had changed; I couldn't afford to travel as my heart desired. However, Cole's expectations for these trips continued, and I still wanted to make those lifelong memories with him. I made it happen by cutting into some of my business budget. (Lesson 1 – DON'T cut the tax payments!) In those years, Cole heard me say, more than once, "Yes, we can do that when the check arrives."

By now, you have surmised that I was not the best money manager. Thank goodness time has brought about many improvements!

My business year two turned to year three, 2001. 9/11 occurred. Immediately, my clients stopped all projects and travel; my work was on hold indefinitely. As a result, I couldn't afford to stay in Hong Kong. Yes, I had a fire sale and sold all my custom-made rosewood furniture, along with everything else possible to get enough money to purchase airplane tickets back to the U.S. for Cole and me.

But where to go and how to continue my career were up in the air. I threw a dart and decided to move to Atlanta, Georgia. I'd reconnected with an old love from my high school days. Between us we had three preteens from our previous marriages.

The U.S. clients were not abundant at that point, but I had work I was finishing up with my Asia-Pacific clients, so I did have some income. However, the checks arrived slowly from Asia. When they didn't arrive as expected, we were compelled to sort out things we no longer needed to own and became regulars at pawn shops to raise cash. We managed to raise enough to buy groceries for a new family of five and have a little left over for a bit of fun for the kids' summer vacation. Thank goodness for Stone Mountain, Georgia. Back then you could fill a car with as many people as it would hold, and the admission fee was seven dollars a day. That place became a life saver!

There were moments we'd say to ourselves, "Do we pay the rent or get rid of the kids?!" I am being facetious but that is how critical it felt from time to time.

My next cash flow crunch came in year nine, 2007-2008. That year marked my biggest NO CASH issue ever.

My husband had joined me in my consulting business. Consequently, we **both** depended on the company's income for the support of our five-person family.

By this time the kids were teenagers, and we had them for summer and winter breaks. Without fail, every time the kids arrived, our client checks didn't! It seemed that the cash always flowed when we had no children in the house, but as soon as they arrived the checks stopped. Cole taught his step-siblings how to watch for the mail. He told them, "When a check arrives, we can (fill in the blank with the desired activity of the day)."

The end of summer was a tortious time for me. Not only were they leaving for months, but we also had to buy the kids school clothes before going back to the other parent. I found myself right there with the kids, praying that checks would arrive in the mail, on time, to pay for the bounty of clothes and shoes for three teens.

Do you get the picture? Lesson 2, "Hope is not a strategy." (Yes, I read that book, and still tried to use that strategy.) What can I say? I'm an eternal optimist, a "high I."

Let's take a break in the story here. To fully explain the lessons of cash flow, I need to explain being a "high I." That is a behavioral style, and it relates to how I managed my money.

The term "High I" is an abbreviation for one of four core styles described in behavioral DISC studies. The terms in DISC have evolved and been reinterpreted many times. While different interpretations use different terminology and visual depictions, the basic tenets of DISC are consistent.

DISC is: Observable behavior, emotions, tone of voice, body language, pace. *It's how we do the things we do.* There are four core behavioral styles: D: Dominance, I: Influence, S: Steadiness, and C: Compliance. There is no right or wrong style. It is your preference for how you do what you do. My preferences may conflict with someone else's preferences, but it doesn't mean I don't like the person; we just have a different preferred approach, and we can *choose* to adapt to someone else's needs.

In my case, I mentioned I was a "high I," Influence. Look at the chart that follows:

Fig. 7-1 Target Training International (TTI) DISC Descriptions

Dominant - How you handle problems/challenges **Influential** - How you handle people & influence others **Steadiness** - How you pace yourself & handle change **Compliant** - How you handle rules & procedures set by others	**"All people exhibit all four behavioral factors in varying degrees of intensity."** - Dr. William Moulton Marston

Recognizing someone's style can allow for better interactions and minimize conflict. The graphic below is a great worksheet for identifying where someone may fall on the DISC profile.

Fig 7-2, TTI's Recognizing DISC Styles

Recognizing DISC Styles

C COMPLIANCE

The "C" is looking for: Information

Emotion: Fear

Quick Observations: Introverted, task-oriented

Communication: Direct

Overextension: Critical

Body Language:
Stance - Arms folded, one hand on chin
Walks - Straight line
Gestures - Very reserved, little or no gestures

Communication Clue: Asks detailed questions

D DOMINANCE

The "D" is looking for: Results

Emotion: Anger

Quick Observations: Extroverted, task-oriented

Communication: Direct

Overextension: Impatient

Body Language:
Stance - Forward leaning, hand in pocket
Walks - Fast, always going somewhere
Gestures - A lot of hand movement when talking, big gestures

Communication Clue: Doesn't want others' opinions, only facts

S STEADINESS

The "S" is looking for: Security

Emotion: Non-emotional

Quick Observations: Introverted, people-oriented

Communication: Indirect

Overextension: Possessiveness

Body Language:
Stance - Leaning back, hand in pocket
Walks - Steady, easy pace
Gestures - Will gesture with hands

Communication Clue: Has a "poker" face

I INFLUENCE

The "I" is looking for: The "Experience"

Emotion: Trust/Optimism

Quick Observations: Extroverted, people-oriented

Communication: Indirect

Overextension: Disorganized

Body Language:
Stance - Feet spread, two hands in pockets
Walks - Weaves, people focused, may run into things
Gestures - A lot of big guestures and facial expressions when talking

Communication Clue: Talks with hands

To understand which style you or others lean towards, answer these two questions:

1. "Am I task-focused or people-focused?"

2. "Am I extroverted (gain more energy when around people), or introverted (gain more energy by being alone with my own thoughts)?"

☐ If you are task-focused and an extrovert, you are referred to as a high D.

☐ If you are task-focused and an introvert, you are referred to as a high C.

☐ If you are people-focused and an extrovert, you are referred to as a high I.

☐ If you are people focused and an introvert, you are referred to as a high S.

If you are still unsure which style you may be, you may have more of a blended style. Look at the following chart. You may find those words better describe you and your combined style.

Fig. 7-3, TTI's Success Insights Wheel ®, Words that Work

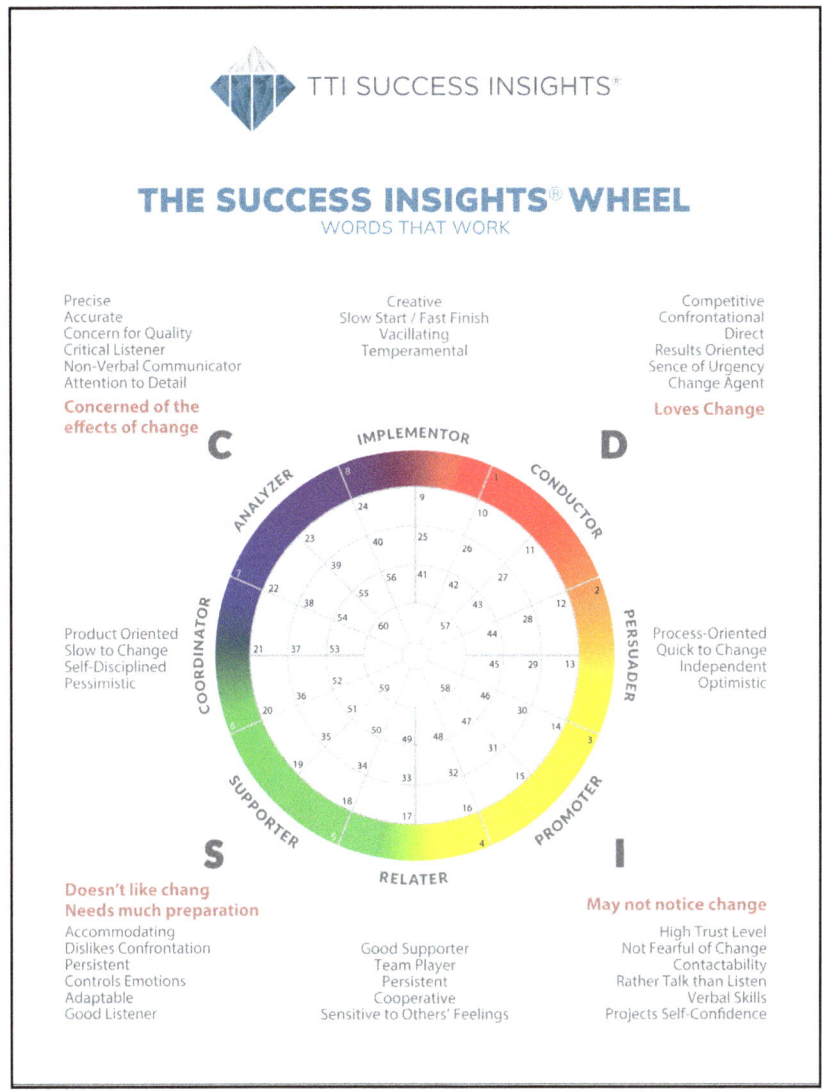

If you would like to identify your specific DISC style, go to chapter 10 for instructions on how to contact me for an online assessment for you or your team.

Referencing the preceding chart, those of you who are organized, detailed, and compliant would **not** have had as many cash flow issues as I had. You would be referenced as a "high C," **analyzer,** whereas I am across the wheel from you, a "high I," **persuader, and promoter,** who pays very little attention to detail, meaning I'm also a "low C."

Here's how I, as a "high I, low C," approached my cash flow. If you recall, I agreed to create my business on a Friday afternoon, and I had incorporated it by the following Monday noon. Business in Hong Kong moves fast, and I had to do the same. I went right to work. I didn't think about my business finances or procuring additional clients for steady income. I had one client; one retainer and a check book; it was enough for me to start my business.

It's difficult for me to disclose my history of poor cash management. But the reason I have shared my experience is that *I do not want you to make the same mistakes.* My desire to avoid you pain and costly errors is higher than my need to look like I had it all together.

Back to where my cash flow story left off. While in Hong Kong, I paid Hong Kong taxes, because I was employed in Hong Kong. You might imagine my surprise when on my return to the States, I filed my US taxes for the first time after living abroad and found out I owed seven years of back taxes. That was a shock and a half! In fact, I thought I had had a bad accountant! That was not the case. In Hong Kong, I had been provided and used accounting services there. The problem was that the complex tax information the accountant recommended simply didn't register with me.

Here is an important point about Behavioral Style "high I, low C." People with my style combination have a difficult time remembering detail or paying attention to detail without support. We are about excitement and spontaneity. International tax law and the intricacies of what had to be paid to whom, at what percentage, depending on the amount of time present in each specific country in Asia Pacific, was too detailed for me to absorb. It did not sink in. I didn't understand the tax structure, or care to study it; I was busy traveling to different countries, doing all kinds of new and exciting things, and having amazing new experiences—which is exactly what makes the "high I" in me TICK! I learned the hard way that when the IRS says you must pay taxes, regardless of the country in which you reside, they are not joking. The U.S. government will send someone to track you down. My advice: plan and pay your taxes.

I'll close my personal cash flow story here. Now let's look at some other ways cash flow can become problematic.

What other cash flow crunches happen to business owners or entrepreneurs?

- **Failure to withhold taxes.** As owners, we can write checks to ourselves. If we are in a hurry, we may not draft the check properly. In those moments we might not pull out proper payroll taxes. If you get behind in payroll taxes, it is nearly impossible to make cash flow cover the shortage. Put the money in separate accounts. Don't get behind the eight ball on this one.

- **Failure to accurately track money.** Create a bookkeeping system that works for you. Do yourself a favor, even if you have very little money, invest in a qualified CPA. They will work with you to teach you QuickBooks or some other online bookkeeping system that you can understand and manage. Don't get caught with your pants down!

- **Not getting your invoices out.** If you don't invoice in a timely manner, you will not see the cash flow on a regular basis. You must have a consistent process for invoicing. (Review Chapter 5 for processes.)

- **Inconsistent bill payment.** Have a consistent process to pay your expenses. In the last few years, I have found the process that keeps my accounting records clean and works for my "low C" preference.

How does cash flow affect **you as the owner, or one of the top** leaders of the organization?

- **Personal self-esteem tends to get tied up with the amount of money you make, affecting your business.** If you're doing well, your self-esteem is strong. You are on top of the world, and you close any client. When money is scarce, you feel like scum of the earth as you scrape pennies together to purchase gasoline to drive to your next client appointment—and that can affect your ability to close that next account.

- **Personal self-esteem and cash flow can affect our image and role of parent in the family.** How do your kids see you? Are you super positive when all goes well, and mean and grumpy when it does not? Please recognize that your value as a human being is not tied to how much money you make. You can be the parent you want to be regardless of your income level.

- **The belief statements you model in your life and with your family can be impacted by your cash flow patterns.** It's a sad mantra if your kids have learned to say, "When the check comes in…." It sets the family dynamic to a dysfunctional mode if your children believe that life goes on hold due to lack of money. Is that a belief statement you want your children to carry throughout their lives? When my son was 29, I heard him say, "When my next check comes in, I'm going to …." I was horrified that I had created his dysfunctional thinking. If I hear him say that now, it triggers me to help him stop that story. If your kids say something similar, help them reframe their statement before it turns into a belief. (Read Chapter 2 on belief statements).

- **You may not be the best person to manage the financial records.** Allow the person with the financial talent to run the books. If both you and your spouse work in the business, it can be very hard on the one who primarily manages the financial planning. It is a heavy burden to keep the family finances in order while also managing the business' cash flow. If you do not have a "high C" (are a detail-oriented individual), but your spouse does, please allow them to do the detail work on the financial books. It will save you thousands of dollars down the road and allow for more harmony and happiness at home. (By the way, you may have to let your ego go. If you have trouble with this you may be operating via a belief statement that says because you are the main owner, you should run the finances.)

- **You must manage your emotional behavior.** Keep your comments and temper in check. What do others hear or see when payroll is tight or short for the week? Does stress rise? Tempers fly? In your anger at seeing your cash fall short, do you make comments under your breath that the company won't survive at this rate?

How does cash flow affect **your team members?**

- If staff overhear you mutter about making payroll, they will be extremely concerned about paying their own bills and keeping their financial commitments. They may assume that their next paycheck is in jeopardy even though you haven't said so. What was venting a little steam to you may cause your team to look for other jobs to ensure they can care for their families. Employees can jump to conclusions and look for new jobs based on your heat of the moment comments.

- The walls have ears and eyes. We think people don't hear us, and we believe that we have said nothing that would give anyone the idea that our cash is in jeopardy, but people in an organization know. They know it by our behaviors and by observing what's going on in the company. They know it by the orders that are not coming in. They understand that few work orders equates to a small amount of cash coming into the company.

- What's going to happen to me? If some people have been laid off, current employees know they could be next. (Review Maslow's Hierarchy of Needs, Chapter 3)

- All of the preceding creates a very unsettled work environment, which in turn leads to lower productivity or absenteeism that affects cash flow.

How does cash flow impact your **current customers?**

- You may not be able to fulfill their orders or provide the services because you have not managed the cash flow properly. The money needed to provide their service or product was tied up doing something else, because you were short and hadn't thought far enough ahead. You borrowed from Peter to pay Paul.

- When you are short on cash, you may use aggressive collection methods. If you want them to pay before your normal payment period, this may irritate or concern customers.

- Customers hear rumors and gossip. If employees are unsettled, it leaks out into the industry and customers ultimately hear it.

I can hear you…enough already! The good news is I've made it through the cash flow crunch several times and finally learned the lessons, and so can you. Let's get to the solutions.

Winning Solution 1: Read *Financial Peace*, by Dave Ramsey. He has the following advice:

- "It's never too late to turn things around, you are the only obstacle."
- "You've got to tell your money what to do or it will leave."
- "Winning at money is 80% behavior and 20% head knowledge."

Thank you, Dave Ramsey for all your lessons in financial peace. If you have not read his books, I urge you to start with *Financial Peace*. He also has written *The Total Money Makeover*, and *EntreLeadership*. They all teach very helpful lessons on strong financial management.

Winning Solution 2: Read *Rich Dad, Poor Dad* by Robert Kiyosaki. He also created a game that we used to play in Hong Kong called

The Cash Flow Game. The principles are easy enough for an eight-year-old to follow. Play it with your family.

Winning Solution 3: Reframe your beliefs. For those of us who grew up with belief statements that said, "Business is hard" or "You can't make money working on your own," it is vital that we reframe our thinking. It is important to get out of our own way and quit making our business harder than it has to be. There are some of us, like me, who think we know better than the IRS. I had to let go of my ego and get out of my own way to do what needed to be done.

Winning Solution 4: Decide who in your organization is going to be responsible for financial management. Have someone else in your organization be a backup. This is vital to any business. If you contract out financial management, you still need someone in your organization to stay engaged and learn the system. Find someone whose behaviors align to that type of work. (Look for someone with a detail-oriented approach, like a "high C.")

Winning Solution 5: Give to get. Those of you who have strong faith may already have the principle of tithing down: first 10% to God, your higher power, or favorite charities and other worthy causes. We reap what we sow. God taught me this principle over and over and continues to teach it to me even now. (I am stubborn).

Many authors and speakers make this point. Look at the following examples:

- **"If you help enough people, you don't have to worry about money."** —Dave Ramsey

- **"We make a living by what we get. We make a life by what we give."** —Winston Churchill

- I am a huge follower of Zig Ziglar: **"You will get all you want in life if you help enough other people get what they want."**

- From a sales standpoint, *The Go Giver* and *The Go Giver Sells More*, by Bob Burg and John David Mann, are wonderful books that show the power of this principle.

Winning Solution 6 and the best one: OK the big finale of what really works. I need a drum roll please. Yes, go ahead Leader, hit the table a couple of times—this is really a big deal!

A few years ago, I ran across Mike Michalowicz's book, *Profit First*. This book is no nonsense. It is perfect for a person with a "high I, low C" style. However, I've seen "high Ds, Ss and Cs" successfully use this method, too. It works. Set up your accounts the way Mike says. You will earn profits, pay your bills on time, AND have money to pay the taxes! Many other winning solutions helped me be successful with cash flow management, but thanks to Mike, I finally broke through my barrier and have joined the financially savvy side. He showed me how to stop robbing Peter to pay Paul and gave me and my family peace of mind.

There is one benefit I *received* from poor cash flow management. It is a stronger and better prayer life. Over the years, I spent a lot of time asking God for help and taking the actions I felt guided to take. My relationship became much stronger as I realized I was being helped. As it says in Matthew 6:26-27 of the New International Version Bible, *"Look at the birds of the air; they do not sow or reap or store away in barns, and yet your heavenly Father feeds them. Are you not much more valuable than they? Can anyone of you by worrying add a single hour (cubit) to your life?"*

 **Moment to Change**

If you're a Dr. Jekyll?	If you're a Mr. Hyde?
• I encourage you to live the go giver principle and find others who can benefit from your wisdom on this subject. • Maybe you could also learn more about behavioral styles.	• There are plenty of things we can stop doing and start doing. • You are probably doing one thing that is helpful, continue doing that!

Whether you are like Dr. Jekyll or Mr. Hyde in regard to cash flow, take a moment to record your thoughts about what you'll do to end the cash flow drama and slay a financial monster (or two).

1. **I'll start doing:**

2. **I'll stop doing:**

3. **I'll continue doing:**

Your spouse now says,

> *"You have done a wonderful job taking care of our finances this year. Even the tax payments were on time. Thank you"*

CHAPTER 8

Lose the Turmoil, Trauma and Drama
Strengthen Leadership & Company Culture

You hear:

> *"The piece that infuriates me the most is when that large order came in. Your two key employees just plain quit. You made all of us go in and work to get that order out. We had to stop our plans to do your employees' work!"*

Leaders, here's the scenario: It suddenly seems like aliens and zombies have taken over your employees' bodies! Who are these people? Your business is in turmoil! Your biggest client has just placed their largest order ever and needs a fast turnaround time. It's a make-or-break moment. How can you make it happen when your employees are completely clueless?

You must deal with the immediate customer crisis, but something is going on with your team, and you just can't quite put a finger on what it is. What the heck has gone wrong? Here is what you are seeing and hearing:

1. Unmotivated and disengaged employees who don't seem to care.

2. Unhappy employees. You heard, "The day-to-day is a drag. It's not fun to work here anymore."

3. Unsure and confused employees. They do tasks that are unimportant and easy, not what needs to be done.

4. Key individuals who leave without even a two-week notice. You overheard them saying, "I can't take it anymore. I'd rather be without a job than work here any longer."

5. Friends you've hired from other parts of your life who do not follow your rules. Instead they make up their own and do whatever they want.

6. Even loyal employees who have stayed through thick and thin seem disgruntled.

7. What drama! You hate drama. The customer order is the last thing on anyone's mind—except yours!

"What kind of monster have I created!?" you might be asking yourself. No time to sort it out right now. You must complete the big order or there won't be a company left!

Halt! Stop the crazies NOW!

Yes, you do have a crisis at hand, and the work must get done. To do that effectively, you must stop the crazies dead in their tracks *now*. It's time to step into your leadership role and clarify the situation. (I don't like to give away answers, as individuals learn best by discovering the truth for themselves, but there is no time to wait! Let's get through this rough spot, then we will step back together and learn.)

Here's the solution to your crisis:

1. Pull the whole place together and have a heart-to-heart talk. You need to own that the company has gotten out of control, and you, as the leader, have things you need to do better. However, right now, you need their help. There is a customer order that must be completed in record time.

2. Tell the group what needs to be done and give them all the dirty details. Tell the whole story.

3. It's time to ask who is in and who is out. Ask for a personal commitment from each one of them. No recourse—you have to see who's in this with you. Anyone not in is politely thanked and asked to leave the company. Yes, it impacts your unemployment percentage, but too bad; take the hit and move on with a team that is committed.

4. Now you have your committed players.

5. Rally the troops around this critical situation of completing this large customer order in record time.

6. How do you rally them? Passionately share your mission and vision for the company. (Use the work you completed or meant to complete from Chapter 2.)

7. Share your newly defined values (from Chapter 3.) If you haven't fully defined them yet, fall back on your personal values for now. Your values reflect how you show up as a leader and will guide the decisions you need to make for this project. It tells the team how you expect them to behave in your organization.

8. Now ask them for their ideas on how to complete this job within the customer's requested timeframe. Determine, as a team, if it is possible to meet that goal.

9. **Listen to them** and take their suggestions. Work together to lay out an action plan you can all agree on. Here's a sample action plan worksheet to track everyone's commitment.

Fig. 8-1, Action Plan

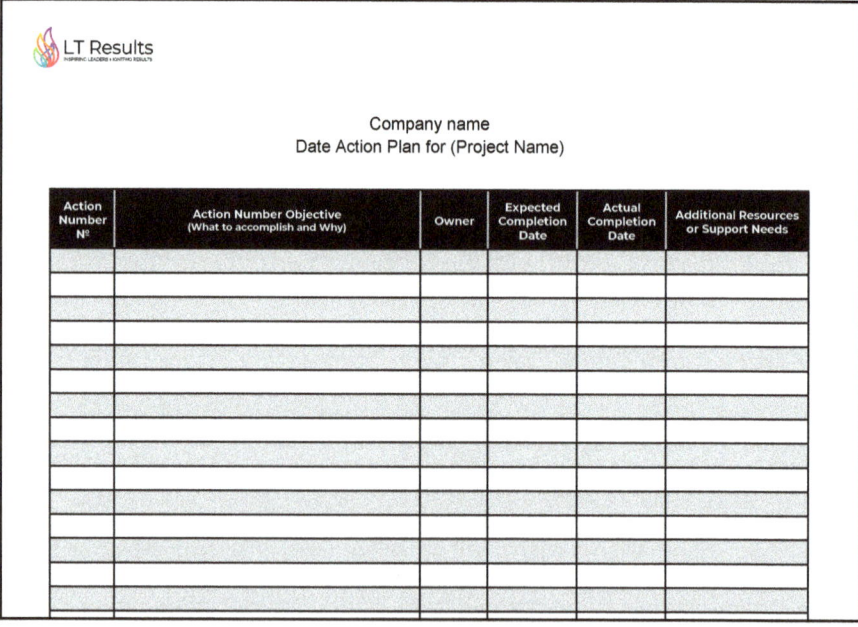

1. Let them help you. Allow them to take the lead and do the jobs you hired them to do. DON'T micromanage.

Delegate properly. (Reference Chapter 5 for steps on How to Delegate.)

2. Use the action plan above or one the team has created. Agree to the frequency of project status checks. Each morning? End of day? Mid-day? Follow the action plan and adjust frequency and details as needed. Keep it up-to-date.

3. Monitor the project. Determine throughout if the team can meet the customer's goal. Inform the customer immediately of any changes to the agreed-to goal. Do not jeopardize your customer relationship by hiding information.

4. If mistakes happen along the way and the timeline is pushed, be truthful with your customer. Own your mistakes and advise the customer how you will remedy the situation. Ask for their consideration with the change of plans. Keep them posted each step of the way with no surprises.

5. Ask the team to advise you if the deadline cannot be met, and to model your behavior by being respectful of everyone's need to know. (Maslow Hierarchy and effective communication, Chapter 4)

WHEW! The crisis is over. The customer's product has been delivered successfully. The team that was left, and a few family members, pulled together and got the job completed. Celebrate and show your appreciation.

Now it is time to fix the company and make good on your promises that things will improve.

Fig. 8-2, Company Culture Survey,

download at: www.LTResults.com/monsterbook/resources

Step 1 – Reflect on reasons the crisis happened and learn. (Evaluate your Company Culture)

Ask yourself these questions and check off all that apply, then tally up your responses to see your results.

- ☐ Do you have unmotivated and disengaged employees?
  - o Are they told they are responsible for carrying out tasks but not given the authority to make it happen?
  - o Have you given them the roles and responsibilities in their positions that you-originally promised?

- ☐ Are your employees unhappy?
  - o Have you heard them say that the day-to-day is a drag?
  - o Do they say they are not having fun?
  - o Remember when we talked about Maslow's Hierarchy of Needs and that people may be at different levels of satisfaction for those needs? Do you know in what levels your employees live right now?
  - o Would you want to work for you? People leave managers not companies.

- ☐ Do you have employees who never take responsibility and are not accountable for the task you assigned them?
  - o Do you ignore that behavior?
  - o Do you address it with them?

- o Do you feel there is never enough time or it's not the right time to address it, so the situation continues to get worse?

- ☐ In other cases when people aren't doing what's been asked, could it be that they don't know how to do it?
  - o Do they know who to ask?
  - o Are they afraid to ask for help?
  - o Is the person who should help available?
  - o Do they know who to go to when you or their manager is not there?

- ☐ Are personal friends whom you've hired treated differently than the rest of the staff?
  - o Do they get special privileges for being part of the "old boys" or "old girls" club?
  - o Are they given special treatment for being part of your church family? Motorcycle group, exercise buddies, etc.?
  - o Do they have seniority?
  - o Are they long-term loyal employees and deemed *untouchable*?

- ☐ Do key people leave unexpectedly.
  - o You've heard, "It's not fun anymore."
  - o "Promises have not been kept."
  - o "I'm not allowed to do the job I was hired to do."

o   "I'm burned out."

SCORING: Tally up how many of these you checked: Total possible points are 26.

Company Culture Survey Results:

26 - 21= The company culture is not healthy. You are not leading. Could you be behaving like Mr. Hyde?

20 - 14 = The company culture is in bad shape. You are not leading consistently. Could you be partly behaving like Mr. Hyde?

13 - 7 = The company culture could use some focus. Dr. Jekyll shows up more than Mr. Hyde.

 0 - 6 = The company culture is in pretty good shape, Dr. Jekyll. What can improve?

Take back control

Now that you've looked at what is happening in your company, let's look at the solutions to take control and get back on track.

As the business owner, leader, and/or entrepreneur, you have two main areas of control:

1.   Your and your team's leadership style and skills.
2.   Your company's culture. This is comprised of the work environment that exists in your company and the attitudes and capabilities of your employees.

We will start with the leadership side of your business, which includes you and others in charge of staff.

LOSE THE TURMOIL PART 1: Your Leadership Style and Skills

You have control over how you come across as a leader. Earlier, I asked, "Would you work for you?" What was your answer?

Have you ever assessed your personal leadership capabilities? If it's been a while since you've done any work on yourself, maybe it's time to set a plan for your (and your team's) leadership development.

> **"The more seriously you take your growth,**
> **the more seriously your people will take you."**
> — John Maxwell

Books are one of the quickest resources for development. (Thank you for reading mine.) There are thousands of leadership books. To help you sort through them, I've listed the top 15 business leadership books of all time in Chapter 10 - References & Resources, from Leaders.com. The concepts in these books are timeless.

The top book on the list is John Maxwell's book, *The 21 Irrefutable Laws of Leadership.*

Here's what I recommend you do with your leadership team. If you're a small business, I encourage you to invite all the staff you've hired to engage them, or if some are uninterested –make it voluntary. (Thanks to Tommy Sinclair, and his leadership reading team, for sharing what they do at Engineered Products.)

Recommended Action 1: Create a Goal for Monthly Leadership Education.

Improve leadership skills by reading books together. We all live busy lives, so it can be difficult to find time for development. Schedule a set time on the company calendar each month to discuss a book the team has selected to read together. It is a wonderful way to learn new concepts and create a group culture of learning. Apply the new learning to what is currently happening in your company.

How to start:

1. Select a book. It could be from the top 15 list or a different one that everyone agrees is important. As the leader, you make the final selection. The company purchases the books for each member who participates.

2. As a group, determine how much time it will take to finish each book. Set the goal for what page or chapter everyone should complete by the next meeting.

3. Meet for one hour, once a month, at the same time each month, if possible. Discuss the book up to the page agreed. Ask questions about the concepts presented, then turn the conversation to how these principles apply in your organization.

4. Jointly agree to the section to be read for next month, or select the next book, and schedule the meeting on the calendar.

5. Be inclusive. Once this begins to take off, check in with the rest of the company from time to time, and invite others to join the leadership reading club. The continuous learning culture will begin to take hold.

Make reading a habit for yourself. It keeps you and your leaders continuously learning and growing.

Recommended Action 2: Plan to assess yourself and your team.

There are many assessments available; some are free online, while others have a fee. I believe any tool that helps you become more self and socially aware is worth its cost and well worth the time invested. You may have already experienced some of the following: Motivators, Acumen, Strength Finders, Myers-Brigg Type Indicator (MBTI), Predictive Index, and DISC behavioral assessments.

A person is much more complex than a single tool can describe. The more a person evaluates and reflects on themselves, the more comfortable and able they will be to lead and mentor others. In previous chapters I've mentioned some of the assessments my business provides through TTI Success Insights. TTI has done extensive research and validation studies with assessments they provide. Following are the results of a peer-reviewed paper "Co-op education and the impact on the behaviors and competencies of undergraduate engineering students," Dr. Nassif E. Rayess, Dr. David Pistrui, Dr. Ron Bonnstetter, and Dr. Eric T. Gehrig, from the 2020 ASEE Virtual Annual Conference, June 22, 2020, https://peer.asee.org/34294 . The paper highlights three important take-aways for leaders.

Bad Bosses Will Affect the Development of Their Team

If a leader is communicating expectations poorly, slacking on communication, or being unkind or unempathetic to their team members, it will affect the short-term work environment and the long-term development of their direct reports, especially younger team members.

All It Takes to Create a Bad Working Environment is No Clarity

More alarmingly, sometimes it doesn't even take a bad boss to cause this lack of development. All it takes is a lack of clarity and understanding. If a new team member enters a role with no expectations laid out for them by leadership, an environment full of conflict and miscommunication will follow.

The good news is that this can easily be avoided by utilizing benchmarking. This process clearly defines expectations and requirements for a role and helps determine the skills necessary for an individual to thrive.

Recognize the Unique Needs of Individuals

Finally, all leaders need to recognize the needs of individuals. Employees are actively looking for bosses that will cultivate their development and help them grow their skills and knowledge. Reports such as TriMetrix DNA provide insights that help both the employee understand self and the employer to provide meaningful and individualized professional development.

Understanding yourself and your team's strengths and areas of development will help you manage with clarity and confidence. Following are additional assessments and some of the questions these tools address. It is not an exhaustive list, but it will give you a place to start establishing development plans for yourself and others:

Assessments Tools:

- *How you do what you do?* A DISC by any provider - TTI, Strength finders, Predictive Index, or MBTI can help you here.

- *Why you do what you do?* A TTI motivating drivers assessment will identify what drives you internally and why you get out of bed in the morning to go to work.

- ***What are your top competency strengths***? TTI's DNA assessment, Strength finders, or Predictive Index can help you identify these.

- *How do you think?* TTI's ACI focuses on a person's clarity in the following dimensions: Understanding Others, Practical Thinking, Systems Judgment, Sense of Self, Role Awareness, and Self Direction. I have not seen another tool that evaluates-these areas. I believe this is critical information to know before hiring or for promotion/succession planning.

- ***How engaged are your employees?*** TTI's Engagement assessment as well as others will help you determine an employee's level of engagement.

- ***Where are your emotional intelligence strengths?*** TTI's Emotional Quotient assessment   address areas based on Daniel Goleman's concepts from his book, *Emotional Intelligence.* The Emotional Quotient Inventory 2.0 (EQ-i-2.0), Profile of Emotional Competence (PEC), The Trait

Emotional Intelligence Questionnaire (TEIQue), Wong's Emotional Intelligence Scale (WEIS), and The Emotional and Social Competence Inventory (ESCI) address EQ.

- *What is your stress level?* TTI's Stress Quotient for individuals and teams or the Stress Mastery Questionnaire will accurately gauge stress.

Surveys:

There is a distinction in the training industry between assessments, which are listed above, and 360- or 180-degree survey feedback tools. For a 360-degree feedback survey, the individual would send survey questions regarding their leadership style to people above them, beside them, below them, and at times to some external, i.e., customers or suppliers. Such a survey is intended to gain insight from the individuals the subject interacts with *around* them, which is why it is called a 360-degree survey. A report comes back with anonymously compiled, candid, objective feedback for the leader. Coaching with the leader is part of the package to ensure the data results are properly interpreted and integrated.

There are numerous providers for these tools, including TTI's Leadership 360 or TEAMS organizational 360-survey, Birkman 360, DDI's Leadership Mirror. They can be ordered standard or customized to align to your company culture. Do research in advance to find the one that best fits your needs.

For further information and details on assessments and surveys, go to Chapter 10 - References & Resources

Recommended Action 3: Self-check with the Jekyll/Hyde Monster Survey

Are you filled with Dr. Jekyll or Mr. Hyde's competencies and skills? Until you can be formally assessed, try this fun, non-validated, unscientific quiz. Though we are having fun with the behaviors of these characters, **the competencies listed are accurate and critical for a leader. Your answers will be a guide for your future development needs.**

Fig. 8-3, How Am I Leading?

Download at: www.LTResults.com/monsterbook/resources

Step 1: Pre-test: Where do you fall on the Jekyll / Hyde scale? Select the box below that best describes your current behaviors.

Throughout the book, I've gone through the success factors for an entrepreneurial business and asked you to check yourself against the behaviors of Dr. Jekyll and Mr. Hyde in each chapter. Where did you land most of the time? Select the box below that best represents your responses prior to taking the quiz that follows.

I am or have...

(Check one)

o Dr. Jekyll: the kindly, professional, high performing leader	o Mostly Dr. Jekyll and a few Mr. Hyde "monster" traits	o Mostly Mr. Hyde "monster" traits, and a few Dr. Jekyll traits	o Mr. Hyde: the unpredictable, disruptive "monster"

Step 2: Rate yourself in the quiz below. Use a 1 – 5 scale to determine where you *really* land. Will you see Dr. Jekyll and Mr. Hyde

behaviors? The competencies that follow are vital in a high performing leader. Be honest regarding your expertise in each area.

Scale: 1 = Poor,   2 = Fair, 3 = Average,   4 = Good,   5 = Excellent

1) Visionary leadership: I see the world differently, help others
    see the vision, and make it a reality.

       1   2   3   4   5

2) Employee development: I facilitate, support, and contribute
    to the professional growth of others.

       1   2   3   4   5

3) Resiliency: I quickly recover from adversity.

       1   2   3   4   5

4) Accountability: I do what I say I'll do, when I say I'll do it (credit to Mike Scott – Vistage Speaker).

       1   2   3   4   5

5) Value-driven decision making: I analyze all aspects of a situation to make consistently sound and timely decisions based on core values.

       1   2   3   4   5

6) Humility: I have little ego and focus more on my teammates than on myself.

       1   2   3   4   5

7) Influence on Others: I personally affect the actions, decisions, opinions, or thinking of others.

       1   2   3   4   5

8) Empathy: I have the ability to understand and share the feelings of another. -

       1   2   3   4   5

9) Visual, verbal, and written communication; My communication is clear and concise, and is demonstrated by my example.

       1   2   3   4   5

10) Teamwork: I ask for help and share credit.

    1   2   3   4   5

11) Delegation: I commit tasks to others with clear instructions and follow-up.

    1   2   3   4   5

12) Conflict Management: I understand, address, and resolve disagreements constructively.

    1   2   3   4   5

13) Optimism: I have hope and confidence about the future and expect successful outcomes.

    1   2   3   4   5

14) Gratitude: I am thankful and appreciative.

    1   2   3   4   5

15) Sense of humor: I have the ability to find things funny and enjoy doing so.

    1   2   3   4   5

HOW TO SCORE: Add up the points you circled for the 15 competencies above and check the box below that applies to your total point score.

Dr. Jekyll: the kindly, professional, high performing leader	Mostly Dr. Jekyll and a few Mr. Hyde "monster" traits	Mostly Mr. Hyde "monster" traits, and a few Dr. Jekyll traits	Mr. Hyde: the unpredictable, disruptive "monster"
75 Total Points	**74 - 36 Points**	**35 - 1 Points**	**0 Total Points**
Terrific! You are a great, high performing leader!	Pretty good. You're on the right track for high performing leader; focus on what you need to improve.	Use that Dr. Jekyll spark and find more opportunities to develop the high performing leader in you.	Would you like to come over from the "dark side"? Follow your chapter action plans and you'll be well on your way to being a high performing leader.

Did your pre-test answer (who you thought you were) match your post-test score (who you really are)? If they are different, what does that tell you? You are correct. You may need to be more self-aware.

Further your development with these ideas:

1. Get a coach and take an assessment or set of assessments.

2. When you do these assessments, I suggest that you buy a debriefing session with the tool to help you understand the report's results and how to apply them to you and your role.

3. Invest in a few additional post-assessment coaching sessions to allow you a safe space to discuss work scenarios and how these tools can help you become a stronger leader. The coach could also help you create a better culture in your organization. (Coming up next in this chapter.)

4. Join a business group of CEO's or leaders as trusted advisors.

5. Read the business books listed in Chapter 10 – References & Resources and start a company leadership reading club.

LOSE THE TURMOIL PART 2: Your Company Culture and How It Impacts Your Team

What is company culture?

The culture of a company is a set of shared core values and practices that define the organization, both internally for employees, and externally as part of its public image. The better defined a company's culture is, the more likely the company will attract top talents who prioritize and share the same values.

Take a moment to reflect on your company's work environment. Write down five words that come to mind to describe your company culture as it exists right now.

1.

2.

3.

4.

5.

Are you happy or satisfied with these words? If not, there are steps you can take to change your culture and make it the one you want.

Company cultures are managed and need a strategy just like sales, finance, operations, and marketing. Have you put any intentional effort into forming your culture?

Those who don't manage their culture see it evolve based on the personalities of the people they employ, as well as the leader. If you don't like the "way people work around here," your culture needs to change. Keep reading, and I'll show you how.

Why is a strong company culture important?

Strong company culture makes work feel exciting and purposeful by enhancing the following areas:

- **Employee engagement**

  Employee engagement is how much employees feel motivated and passionate about the work they do. A strong company culture encourages employees to feel committed to their work by creating a community of like-minded individuals driven by similar principles and values. Employees who are more engaged with their work are also more likely to relate to each other and solve problems effectively.

- **Productivity**

  Employees are most productive when they feel like valued members of the team. A strong culture creates a diverse, inclusive workplace where employees feel their contributions matter. This sense of value can increase productivity and lead to consistent output and better results overall.

- **Talent retention**

  Workers who enjoy their company and its culture are more likely to remain there longer. This can also increase a company's external reputation as it becomes known for being a workplace where employees want to stay and grow. Employees like to be hired by "best places to work" organizations.

In the early days of my DHL Worldwide Express career, we called the corporate culture esprit de corps . Do any of you remember or use that phrase?

You may be wondering, what the heck is esprit de corps? It is the *common spirit* existing in the members of a group that inspires enthusiasm, devotion, and strong regard for the honor of the group.

For genuine esprit de corps to develop you must have a conscious intention to focus on your team's culture. Dividends include— but are not limited to—increased motivation, higher employee engagement, improved results, and a real sense of fun, worth, and belonging.

The military branches are a wonderful reflection of this in action. One can hear the pride and protection each branch feels and declares for their brothers and sisters in arms. I see it in my husband's comradery after 20 years of retirement from the US Coast Guard with those he served alongside. It is truly amazing to see the love and affection they have for one another, demonstrated by inside jokes, shared experiences of on-duty stories and memories of places they lived and traveled.

Fig. 8-4 Develop Esprit de Corps

To Develop Esprit de Corps Means Investing the Time to

- Know your team members — truly know them as people, not as just people who complete tasks.
- As a leader be personal, talk about what the group means to you and don't be afraid to show vulnerability. Show personal appreciation.
- Set high standards for the group and follow up on those.
- Understand that morale is extremely important and dedicate the time to create, foster and maintain this.
- Create a sense of unique identity. I once gave my team a name unique to us and printed black business cards for every member with our name on it. I reminded them the name symbolized who we were and what we stood for in terms of standards and this was a physical reminder. 10 years later a member took a picture of that card in his wallet.
- Always maintain open communication.
- Provide support to all members of your team.
- Tell your team a story. Tell them where we are today, where we want to be; the part they can play, and what is in it for them. (That is sharing your why, the purpose and vision of the company and their roles in the organization)
- Create a siege (a reason to fight together) or a themed goal - a customer project - Be competitive — tell your team you want to outperform other teams/competitors— light the fire and talk about it.
- Always communicate — prioritize and make the time to communicate all the time — people want to know what is happening where they work.
- Have fun. Both in work and out of work — shared experiences and shared laughter and jokes are the glue that keeps a team together and reminds them of the human interactions and connections that have been formed.

2000 Harvard Business Review, entitled 'Let's Put More Esprit in de Corporation', on 2.11.2019, Martin Teasdale

In a *Harvard Business Review* article, "Let's Put More Esprit in de Corporation," February 11, 2019 , Martin Teasdale reported that B. Houston discussed what he perceived to be signs of strength and health in a company. Of the various factors he identified, esprit de corps was at the top of the list.

I'd encourage you to resurrect the use of esprit de corps as part of *your* company culture. The list that follows describes how to create that common spirit. It echoes many of the things we've already discussed.

Now, let's think back to your raging crisis at the start of this chapter. One of the reasons your team may have gone off the rails is that you had not yet developed an accountability chart for the organization, or it had changed significantly from when you first developed it. (See Chapter 2 for how to do this). You may have lost staff, others have stepped in to help out, or roles may not have been filled.

Remember, an effective corporate culture must address:

1. Retention of your staff.
2. Engagement of your staff.
3. Productive work for staff.

Let's start with productive work. If your employees productively contribute their talents and capabilities to the business, their personal whys are aligned and connected to your company's why. When employee and company connect, you keep the employee engaged. Engaged employees become loyal employees who don't want to leave your business because they are happy and fulfilled, which is now an accurate description for your company culture.

Let me help you nail this concept down to ensure it takes root in your company. There is another set of Zenger-Miller key actions that work well for this situation: *Fig. 8-5 Key Actions for Clarifying team roles and responsibilities* to ensure your employees are committed and engaged. Before you meet with your employees, I suggest you plan ahead, gather your leaders, and answer these questions from your organization's perspective.

Planning Questions:

- What is the team's purpose and impact on the organization?

- What results and standards do you expect this team to achieve?

- What do you know about each team member's strengths, preferences, and development needs?

- What resources do you expect the team to use?

Once you have considered your answers, hold a meeting for the entire company. Conduct the meeting confidently; use these key actions as your agenda points:

*Fig. 8-5: **Key Actions for Clarifying Team Roles and Responsibilities:***

Key Actions for Clarifying Team Roles and Responsibilities

1. Explain the team's purpose and impact on the organization.
2. Describe the results and standards the team is expected to achieve.
3. Discuss and agree on the roles and responsibilities of each team member.
4. Identify procedures and resources for getting the work done.
5. Encourage team members to figure out and agree on ways to help each other.
6. Summarize and establish a specific follow up plan.

1. **Explain the team's purpose and impact on the organization.**

2. **Describe the results and standards you expect the team to achieve.**

3. **Discuss and agree on the roles and responsibilities of each team member.** *(You could place their names on Post-it notes on the organizational accountability chart for visual support and documentation. Sample chart in Chapter 2).*

4. **Identify procedures and resources for getting the work done.** *(Refer to processes created from Chapter 5. If you have not yet done this, it can be a project to build esprit de corps by getting staff to work together and document these processes.)*

5. **Encourage team members to discuss and agree on ways to help each other.** *(Create ground rules and operating agreements.)*

6. **Summarize and establish a specific follow-up plan.** *(Use the blank action form from Fig. 8-1 as a tool).*

BRAVO! The team is charged up and ready to go.

Team Development Stages and DISC Behaviors

When teams initially come together, they are **forming**. If you followed the steps above, You, the leader, just reset this group and helped them **form** a newly established team with new expectations, clear role alignment, and operating agreements.

Know that *there will be predictable conflict* that builds within the team. Bruce Tuckman created a team development model, and in that model Stage 2 of development is referred to as **storming**. Distrust and knowledge hoarding begins. Misunderstandings and disagreements occur. This is where the differences in DISC styles clearly show up. In most cases, arguments and disagreements happen because actions and words are misinterpreted and arguments escalate.

To illustrate, consider this: D's like conflict, S's don't. C's like details and proof, I's don't. I's want to be center stage and noticed, no matter the issue. With those kinds of dynamics going on, you're going to have a few disagreements to manage! Conducting team-alignment workshops is especially effective during team development stages. See Chapter 10 - References & Resources for how to schedule one of these.

Fig. 8-6: DISC Styles and How They Approach Conflict:

Conflicts are not a bad thing. The tension that builds can produce creativity and innovation as people work together to find solutions to meet the diverse needs of everyone. Don't be afraid to let a team argue—as long as their temperaments stay respectful and productive.

Once the team is aligned and begins to trust one another, they move into the **norming** phase of development; collaboration and sharing knowledge occurs. Some teams stay in this space quite some time and never move to **performing**. Conversely, others move quickly to performing where they create knowledge and are in sync.

Fig. 8-7, Bruce Tuckman, Team Development - additions

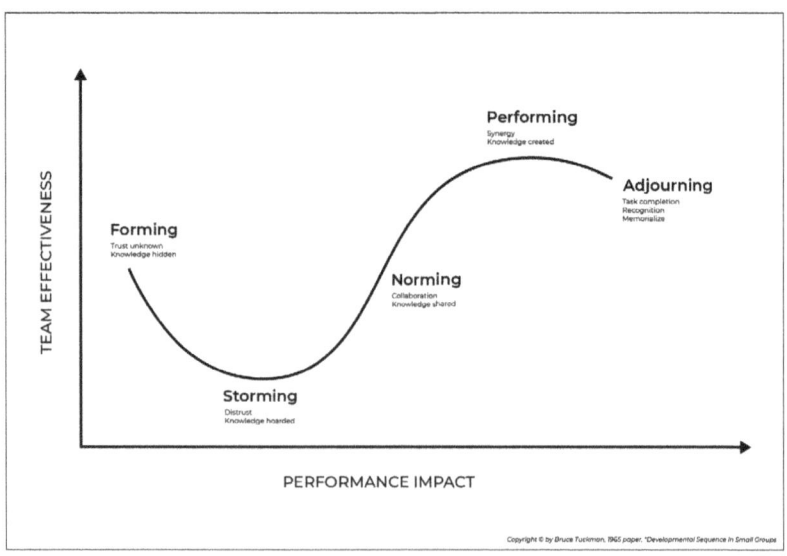

Anytime someone joins or leaves the team, the team falls back into **forming and storming** and needs to re-establish. Refocusing the team, incorporating ground rules, and understanding one another's styles will help the team move faster through the stages back to **norming.**

Reinforcing esprit de corps and community, sharing expectations, and working on joint projects will help drive the team into **performing.** Here they create knowledge and are in sync with one another.

Again, if at some point while they are **performing**, a person joins or leaves the team, the team goes back to **forming** and will proceed through the development stages again. It may be very quick, but they have to regroup.

When the team is no longer working together for whatever reason, it is **adjourning.** To properly close a team, acknowledge the ending, recognize the work and effort that had been accomplished, and in some way memorialize the team. That's living esprit de corps!

Components of Company Culture

A few more points before we wrap up company culture. What defines a good company culture?

Each company or organization is unique in its approach to the work and the values that bring them together. Good company culture is *consistent* and *authentic* to those *specific values*. It's important to create a strategy for your culture, just like sales, finance, and operations. You'll see from the following list that much of your work will already be planned or underway from your earlier assignments in this book.

Components of Company Culture

- Shared mission, vision, and values

- Relationship between leadership and employees— communication methods
- Employee acknowledgement of achievement—awards and recognition
- Professional development—inhouse or external development
- Aesthetics and atmosphere—appearance, dress code, social calendar

What about those five words you wrote down or thought about to describe your culture a few pages back? If you were to intentionally create the culture, what words would you use?

1.

2.

3.

4.

5.

If you'd like to go deeper and set fundamentals in place for your culture, I highly recommend reading *Culture by Design: 8 Simple Steps to Drive Better Individual and Organizational Performance* by David Friedman. Why reinvent the wheel? This is a wonderful book to further explain how to a create company culture that sticks. I've worked with the author and this is quality process. He has also created an app to use within your organization that makes it very effective.

"Customers will never love a company until the employees love it first."
—Simon Sinek, author, Start with Why

Key points from this chapter:

- Steps to work through a crisis.

- Reasons why your raging crisis occurred. The Company Culture quiz.

- Lose the Turmoil - Solutions you can control:

1) Your leadership style & skills

  - Top 15 leadership books & potential book club.

  - Plan to self-assess.

  - Self-check with The Dr. Jekyll/ Mr. Hyde Monster Quiz.

2) Your company culture

  - Elements to watch: employee engagement, valued productivity, and retention.

  - How to create esprit de corps—focus on your team's culture.

  - Key actions to clarify team roles and responsibilities.

- Team development stages: Forming, Storming, Norming, Performing, Adjourning.

- How to manage conflict for each DISC style.

- Five words to describe your company's culture—are they what you want?

 **Moment to Change**

Where did you land on the Dr. Jekyll or Mr. Hyde scale?

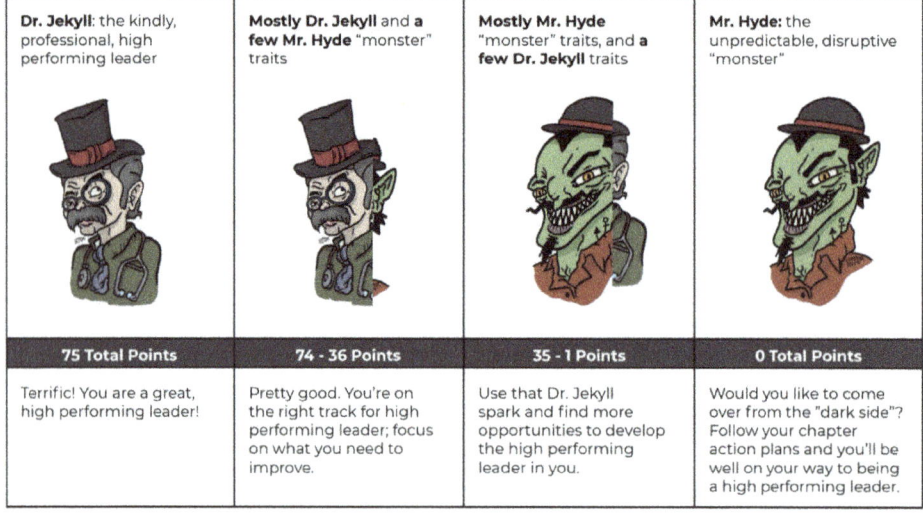

Dr. Jekyll: the kindly, professional, high performing leader	Mostly Dr. Jekyll and a few Mr. Hyde "monster" traits	Mostly Mr. Hyde "monster" traits, and a few Dr. Jekyll traits	Mr. Hyde: the unpredictable, disruptive "monster"
75 Total Points	**74 - 36 Points**	**35 - 1 Points**	**0 Total Points**
Terrific! You are a great, high performing leader!	Pretty good. You're on the right track for high performing leader; focus on what you need to improve.	Use that Dr. Jekyll spark and find more opportunities to develop the high performing leader in you.	Would you like to come over from the "dark side"? Follow your chapter action plans and you'll be well on your way to being a high performing leader.

Whether Dr. Jekyll or Mr. Hyde, you know there is always plenty you can do to keep turmoil from impacting your corporate culture. Lead your way out of it!

1. What will you start doing from this chapter?

2. What will you stop doing?

3. What will you continue doing?

"Corporate culture is the only sustainable competitive advantage that is completely within the control of the entrepreneur."
—David Cummings, Co-Founder, Pardot

Your spouse now says:

> *"I would be delighted to go to your team dinner. They all seem to get along so well and love their jobs."*

Who wins out in the next chapter? Dr. Jekyll or Mr. Hyde?

CHAPTER 9

"Stay the Course" - Follow through with Action Plans

Dear Leader, where did you end up last chapter? More like Dr. Jekyll or Mr. Hyde?

If you had traits of both, you are not alone. Life is about lessons and growth, and as business owners / entrepreneurs we get to play out our lessons in public for all the world to see. Many of us want the world to see us in a certain light. Some like to be referenced as entrepreneurs while others prefer business owners. It comes down to *your beliefs* of who and what those titles represent to you.

As I proceed with this chapter I want to share *my belief* about those titles. Whether you consider yourself a business owner or an entrepreneur, in *my beliefs* anyone who owns a business has certain traits, be it a startup or a multi-million dollar enterprise. The following entrepreneurial traits apply to you who own businesses.

"An entrepreneur tends to bite off a little more than they can chew hoping they'll quickly learn how to chew it." — Roy Ash

Let that sink in for a moment. It's true. *You* are one of the mavericks. You don't wait until you have it all figured out before you step in to start. You jump in and hit the ground running. How else do you make a splash before the competition?

Business owners/entrepreneurs can emerge at any stage of life, from any realm. There are many kinds of personality types and every range of grade point averages. Every owner is unique, but there are two key traits that stand out. Owners persist with stick-to-it-iveness, like a dog with a bone. They persist until they have exhausted all ways to solve a problem, only to reset and come back with yet another plan of action. Secondly, they have an uncanny ability to take risks while also managing fear and uncertainty.

A third trait you, as owners/entrepreneurs have, is a desire for your businesses to make a difference in the lives of those around you and ultimately have an impact on the world. That kind of passion rubs off on others. Magic happens when you, as leaders, share your passion, broadcast it, and inspire others to become part of your vision, too.

A single book, even this one, will not make monster issues totally disappear from your business. However, it *will* tame them and make them more manageable if you consistently follow your action plans and stay the course.

Becoming an overnight sensation takes time. It could take years or even decades of slogging through successes and failures, taking two steps forward and one step back. It is your stick-to-it-iveness and belief in yourself and your ideas that will make others think you're an overnight success.

We owners are motivated by other owners/entrepreneurs' success (and their quotes). We love to collaborate and share best practices, so we don't have to learn every hard lesson personally. We read biographies, watch *Shark Tank* and *Undercover Boss*, listen to the latest podcasts, and integrate the latest business book's concepts into our organizations. When we're not in our business physically, we are there mentally.

In this book, one of my goals was to help you see your blind spots. You now realize not everyone is wired the same as you. Your employees want time with you. Your customers want time with you. Your spouse and families want time with you, too. The ability to **balance your time** will be one of the hallmarks of your success.

Applying the concepts in this book will give you **Freedom.** The concepts free you up to spend time where you want to spend your time, and not have to be chained to your business. I encourage you to integrate Maslow's Hierarchy of Needs into your psyche. It will help you interact and connect more deeply with others and provide you greater fulfillment.

Where to start?

1. Your first step is to ensure your foundation is solid. How? Go to Chapter 2 and document your Mission, Vision and Organizational Chart.

2. Then to Chapter 3 to commit to your values. If you have completed the actions and suggestions in those chapters, identify the next most important issue and address it before it becomes a monster.

The **secret is**… stay the course and follow up to **implement and execute** your actions. Then you will see your goals realized.

"A clear purpose will unite you as you move forward, values will guide your behavior, and goals will focus your energy."
—Kenneth H. Blanchard

What's the Future Hold?

"The best way to predict the future is to create it."
—Peter Drucker

Leader, fast forward – 2 years from today

Your spouse says:

> *"You got what in the mail?*
> *An invitation to accept your award as Business*
> *Owner of the Year?*
> *I am so proud of you!"*

Congratulations on achieving **Business Owner of the Year**!

Two years ago, you and your leadership team identified the most important things to accomplish in your business. Your planning had revealed a gap. The leadership team needed to see the solutions for success on one page to prioritize and determine the focus for each month.

You found the "**High Performing Checklist** from the 9 Solutions to Conquer the "Monstrous" Challenges in Your Business" a perfect tool. It outlined the factors and Jekyll/Hyde behaviors, which allowed you to track and implement SOLUTIONS throughout the year. This way you ensured that you and your team addressed your company's blind spots.

Each month, you reprioritized your focus on the solution factor that needed the most attention. You reflected on the triggers for each factor, so you could be conscious of your desired actions and potential reactions. This allowed you to lead the team successfully with few negative consequences. Your goal was to be like Dr. Jekyll, although Mr. Hyde behaviors still showed up, but much less frequently than before.

The Jekyll/Hyde duality of behavior has become an inside joke in your company, part of your culture. It has become a gentle reminder when tensions rise: "Don't behave like Mr. Hyde!" Just speaking Mr. Hyde's name has become an immediate cue for leaders and team members to step away and de-stress.

Yes, two years ago you reviewed and updated your mission, vision, and values to better reflect who you are. The organization began to grow faster. You kept close watch on the roles and responsibilities of all the team members to scale the organization appropriately. Now you strategically hire and delegate to new leaders. Loyalty has increased and the number of retained staff has grown. Your company's corporate culture now reflects caring, engagement, and esprit de corps—thanks to your guidance, transparency, and leadership.

Processes have been established and are followed. Leaders and employees are engaged and collaborate. Mini teams formed on the spot to address special projects. Individual team members discovered their strengths and their preferred working styles to enable better collaboration. Now when "storming" erupts in a team, the members are aware; they diagnose and correct their behaviors quickly by adapting their own DISC style to others.

Teams have reached high performing status more quickly than ever, and synergy abounds with the creation of new ideas and processes.

In this new, fast-paced work environment stress builds from time to time, but Mr. Hyde behaviors are fewer and farther between. Your company even created a partnership with the exercise and yoga studio next door; staff visit throughout the day to keep their emotional edges down and energy high.

Last year you overcame the last big hurdle. The cash flow crunch FINALLY went away. You focused on the "give-to-get principle," and straightened out your accounts –budgeting for long-term expenses. By the end of the year you were able to reward the team with bonuses for the first time in the company's history. The joy could be felt throughout the organization.

Speaking of joy, that was one of the five words you listed two years ago when you set new intentions for your company culture. You continue to refine your culture strategy to build on the results you now see and feel.

This year the business focus is for the next level of leadership development and cross-functional team development. You have begun a mentorship program for underprivileged students to give back to your community, and have found innovative ways to interact with customers who have supported you.

In your acceptance speech, you shared that your secret tool for success was a "High Performing Checklist" that allowed you to get your business back on track and ultimately enabled you to be recognized as Business Owner of the Year.

Congratulations!

My Leader Friends, I'm rooting for you! Use the High Performance Checklist and solutions in this book to tame your business monsters and get back on track—so that *you'll* be the next Business Owner of the Year!

Good Luck! Enjoy *Your* Quest!

High Performance Checklist
9 SOLUTIONS TO CONQUER THE "MONSTROUS" CHALLENGES IN YOUR BUSINESS

What's the status of yours?

Monster Chapter	Solution Factor	Danger	Caution	Working	Am I Dr. Jekyll	Am I Mr. Hyde	Both at times?
	Shared Mission & Vision	○	○	○	☐	☐	☐
	Organizational Chart Roles & Responsibilities	○	○	○	☐	☐	☐
	Link to Values Beliefs turn into Actions	○	○	○	☐	☐	☐
	Understand & Engage Know Others' Needs	○	○	○	☐	☐	☐
	Top Chaos Creators Processes to Restore Calm	○	○	○	☐	☐	☐
	In Control of Stress & Emotions	○	○	○	☐	☐	☐
	On Top of Cashflow Give to Others	○	○	○	☐	☐	☐
	No More Turmoil Leadership & Culture	○	○	○	☐	☐	☐
	Stay the Course! Use Action Plans	○	○	○	☐	☐	☐
THIS MONTH:	Our Focus is:	○	○	○	☐	☐	☐

LT Results and Mouth-agape.com

CHAPTER 10

Quick Reference & Resources

This chapter is for easy reference. These are the tools that I introduced and shared within the book. I am listing them by the chapter they were introduced. I know some of you just want the tools, if so, this will be your favorite chapter. Download pdf files at: **www.LTResults.com/monsterbook/resources**

For information and details about Team events, access to "reader-priced" assessment links or surveys please email Liz@LTResults.com with your request.

Resources from Chapter 2: **Remember Why You Started this Business** —Set a Shared Mission and Vision for Organizational Clarity

Resources from Chapter 2: **Remember Why You Started this Business** —Set a Shared Mission and Vision for Organizational Clarity

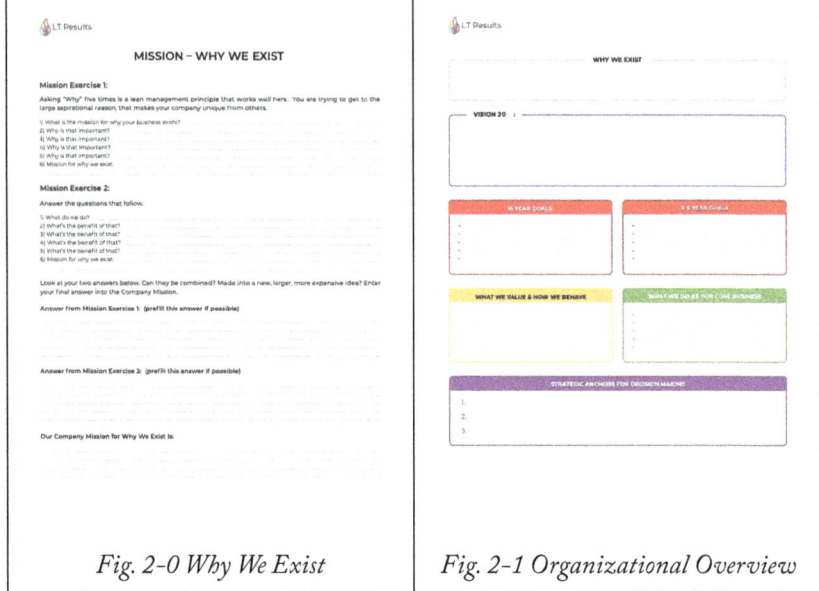

| Fig. 2-0 Why We Exist | Fig. 2-1 Organizational Overview |

Resources from Chapter 2: **Remember Why You Started this Business** —Set a Shared Mission and Vision for Organizational Clarity

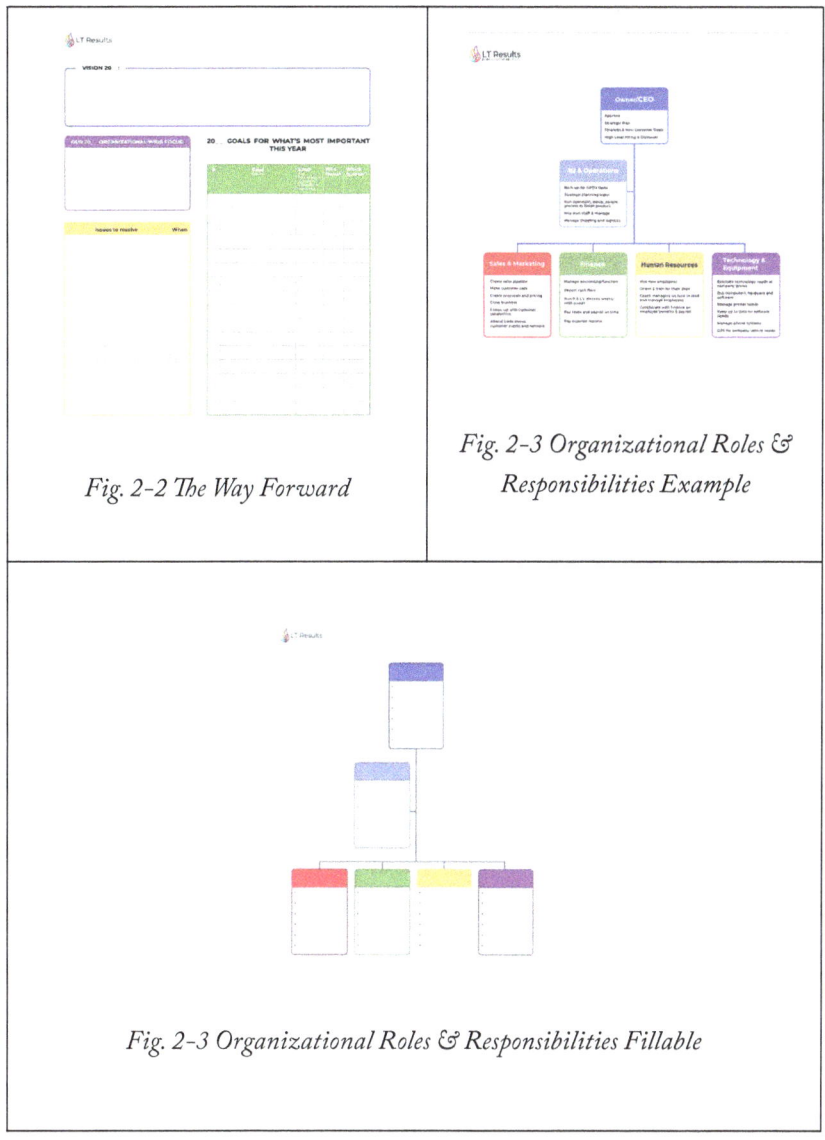

Fig. 2-2 *The Way Forward*

Fig. 2-3 *Organizational Roles & Responsibilities Example*

Fig. 2-3 *Organizational Roles & Responsibilities Fillable*

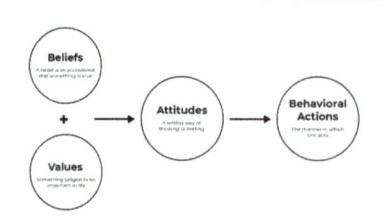

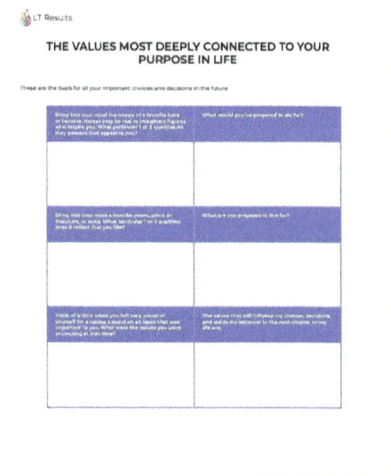

Here are a couple exercises to do to uncover your values:

1.Think about the people you have fired in the past. What were they fired for?

2.Write down those reasons and identify the pattern. Most likely it reveals the values that you hold dear. Those are your values.

3.Think about when someone offends you. Which of your values did they violate?

Fig. 3-1 Beliefs and Values Drive Behaviors

Fig. 3-2 Values Most Deeply Connected to Your Purpose in Life

Resources from Chapter 4: **Do I show I care?** Understand and Engage Others

From Featured Masterclass Instructor, Robin Arzón:

In a 1943 paper titled "A Theory of Human Motivation," American psychologist Abraham Maslow theorized that human decision-making is undergirded by a hierarchy of psychological needs. In his initial paper and a subsequent 1954 book titled Motivation and Personality, Maslow proposed that five core needs form the basis for human behavioral motivation.

Maslow referred to self-actualization as a "growth need," and he separated it from the lower four levels on his hierarchy, which he called "deficiency needs."

According to his theory, if you fail to meet your deficiency needs, you'll experience harmful or unpleasant results. Conditions ranging from illness and starvation up through loneliness and self-doubt are the byproduct of unmet deficiency needs.

By contrast, self-actualization needs can make you happier, but you are not harmed when these needs go unfulfilled. Thus, self-actualization needs only become a priority when the other four foundational needs are met first.

Fig. 4-1 Theory of Maslow's Hierarchy

Fig. 4-2 Maslow's Hierarchy of Needs

Fig. 4-3 How to Show Care Using Maslow's Hierarchy of Needs

Basic Principles

1. Focus on the situation, issue, or behavior, not on the person.
2. Maintain the self-confidence and self-esteem of others.
3. Maintain constructive relationships with your employees, peers, and managers.
4. Take initiative to make things better.
5. Lead by example.

Copyright © 1996 by Zenger Miller

Fig. 4-4 The Basic Principles

Resources from Chapter 5: **Am I a Chaos-Creator?** Top Business Processes to Restore Calm

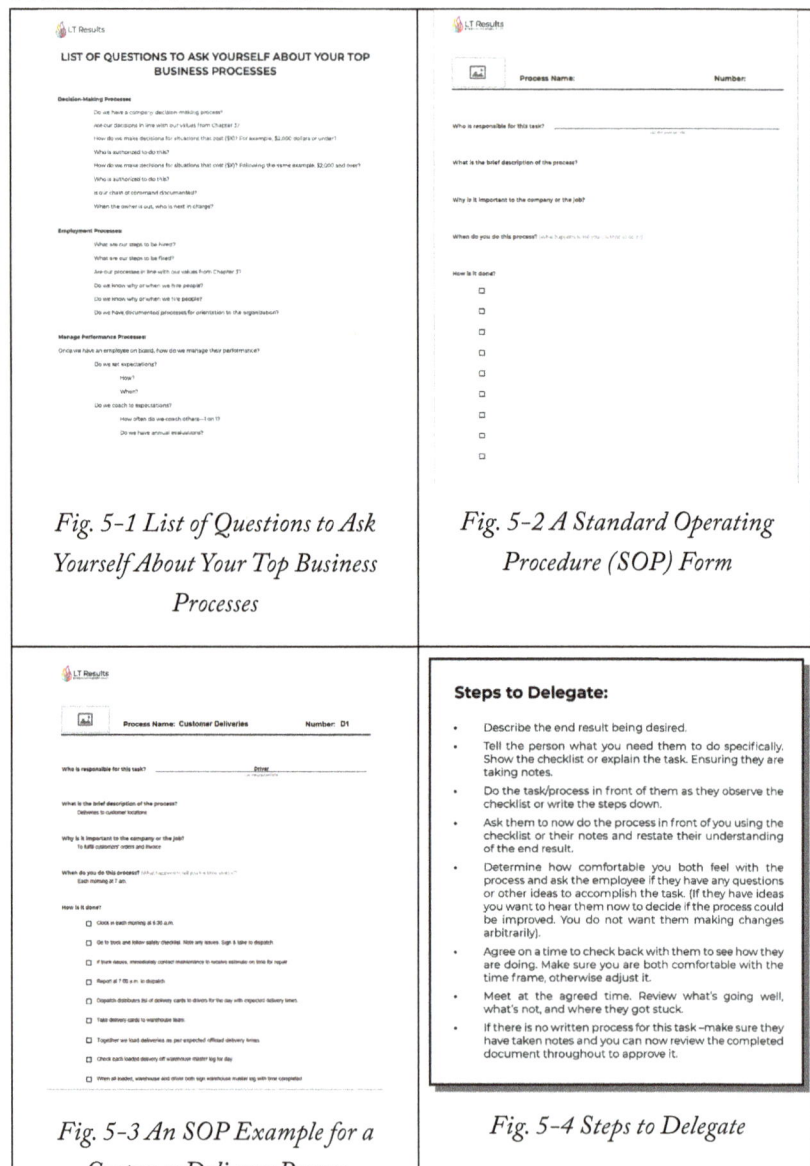

Fig. 5-1 List of Questions to Ask Yourself About Your Top Business Processes

Fig. 5-2 A Standard Operating Procedure (SOP) Form

Fig. 5-3 An SOP Example for a Customer Delivery Process

Fig. 5-4 Steps to Delegate

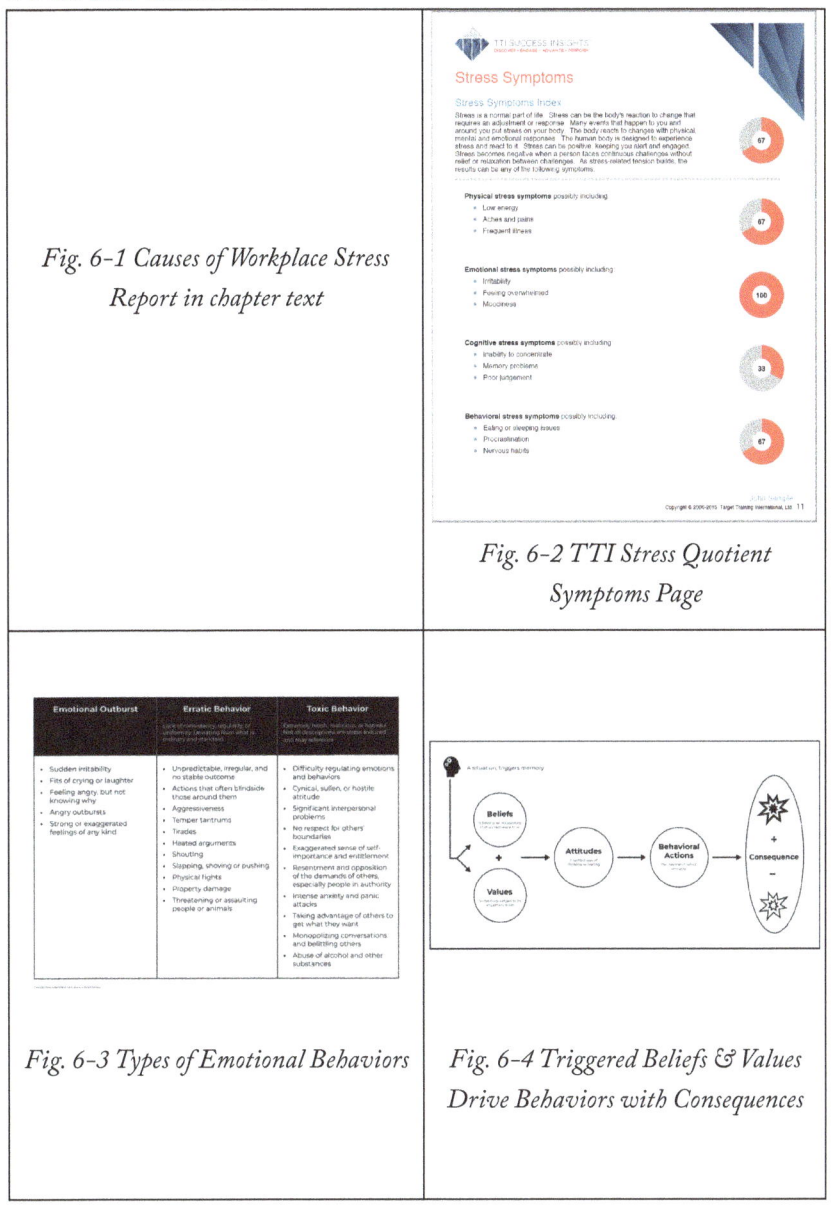

Fig. 6-1 Causes of Workplace Stress Report in chapter text

Fig. 6-2 TTI Stress Quotient Symptoms Page

Fig. 6-3 Types of Emotional Behaviors

Fig. 6-4 Triggered Beliefs & Values Drive Behaviors with Consequences

The Key Actions for Emotional Behavior are:

1. Calmly acknowledge the emotional behavior.
2. Describe the impact the emotional behavior is having on you and on the discussion.
3. Determine if it's possible to continue the discussion constructively.
4. Propose an approach for jointly re-focusing on the work issue.
5. Express support and reassurance.

The key actions for emotional behavior are:

1) Calmly acknowledge the emotional behavior. (Use the phrase, "You look…(emotion)". If not sure, use, "You look (mad), (sad), or (glad), they will correct you with the proper emotion.)

2) Describe the impact the emotional behavior is having on you and on the discussion. (It upsets me when you're (emotion) as I can't keep my focus on the discussion in the team meeting.)

3) Determine if it's possible to continue the discussion constructively. (Are we able to continue this conversation now or do you need some to collect yourself?)

4) Propose an approach for jointly re-focusing on the work issue. (In the future, what if, when this topic comes up…)

Fig. 6-5 The Key Actions for Emotional Behavior

Fig. 6-6 TTI Emotional Quotient ™ Dimensions

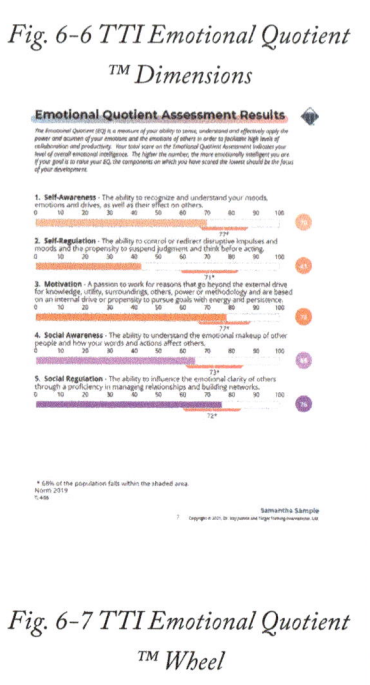

Fig. 6-7 TTI Emotional Quotient ™ Wheel

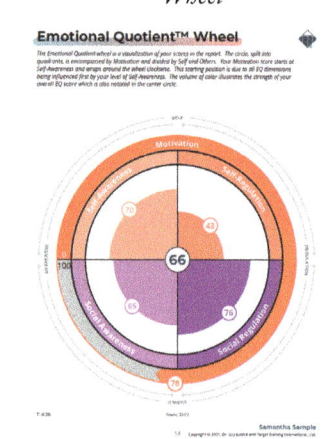

Resources from Chapter 7: Cash Flow Crunch! Get On Top of Cash Flow

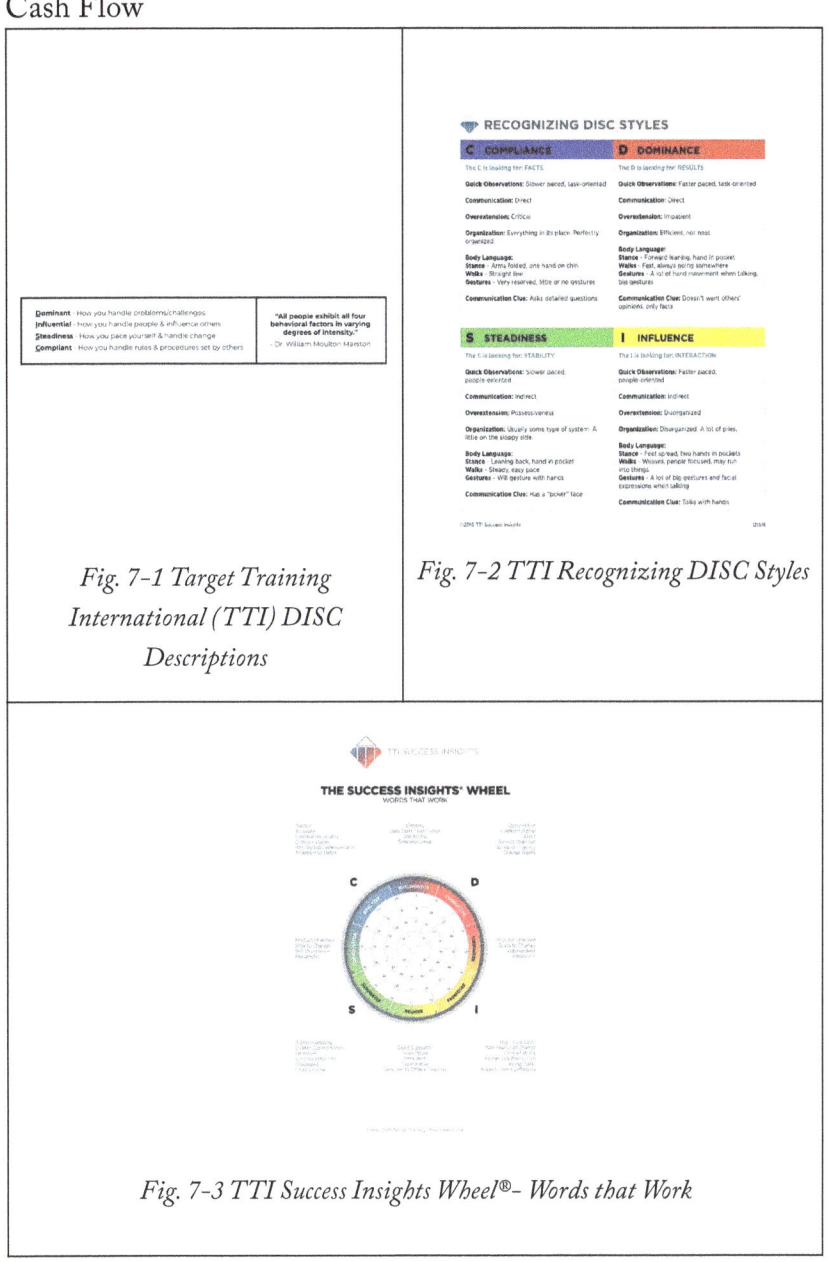

Fig. 7-1 Target Training International (TTI) DISC Descriptions

Fig. 7-2 TTI Recognizing DISC Styles

Fig. 7-3 TTI Success Insights Wheel®- Words that Work

Resources from Chapter 8: **Lose the Turmoil, Trauma and Drama**
Strengthen Leadership & Company Culture

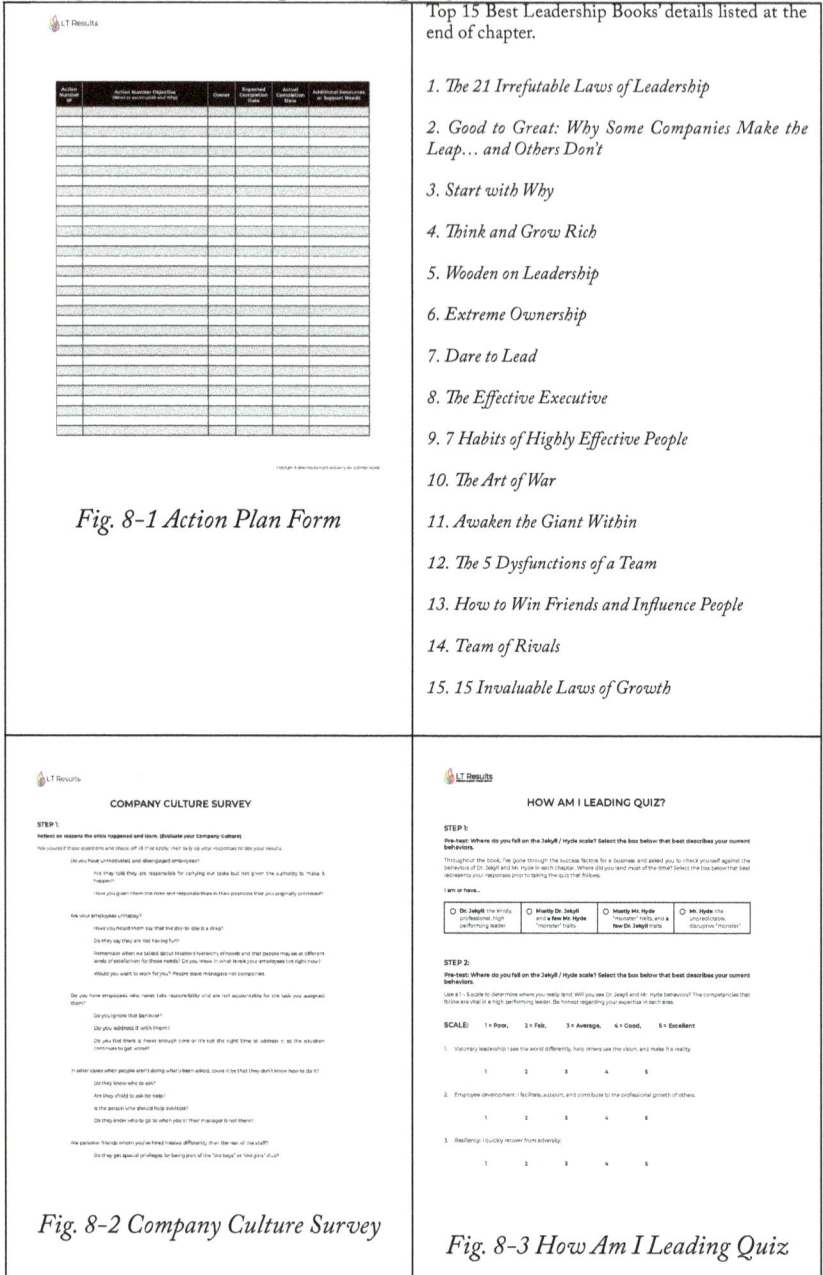

Top 15 Best Leadership Books' details listed at the end of chapter.

1. *The 21 Irrefutable Laws of Leadership*

2. *Good to Great: Why Some Companies Make the Leap… and Others Don't*

3. *Start with Why*

4. *Think and Grow Rich*

5. *Wooden on Leadership*

6. *Extreme Ownership*

7. *Dare to Lead*

8. *The Effective Executive*

9. *7 Habits of Highly Effective People*

10. *The Art of War*

11. *Awaken the Giant Within*

12. *The 5 Dysfunctions of a Team*

13. *How to Win Friends and Influence People*

14. *Team of Rivals*

15. *15 Invaluable Laws of Growth*

Fig. 8-1 Action Plan Form

Fig. 8-2 Company Culture Survey

Fig. 8-3 How Am I Leading Quiz

214

To Develop Esprit de Corps Means Investing the Time to

- Know your team members — truly know them as people, not as just people who complete tasks.
- As a leader be personal, talk about what the group means to you and don't be afraid to show vulnerability, show personal appreciation.
- Set high standards for the group and follow up on those.
- Understand that morale is extremely important and dedicate the time to create, foster and maintain this.
- Create a sense of unique identity. I once gave my team a name unique to us and printed black business cards for every member with our name on it. I reminded them the name symbolized who we were and what we stood for in terms of standards and this was a physical reminder. 10 years later a member took a picture of that card in his wallet.
- Always maintain open communication.
- Provide support to all members of your team.
- Tell your team a story. Tell them where we are today, where we want to be, the part they can play, and what is in it for them. (That is sharing your why, the purpose and vision of the company and their roles in the organization)
- Create a siege (a reason to fight together) or a themed goal - a customer project - Be competitive — tell your team you want to outperform other teams/competitors— light the fire and talk about it.
- Always communicate — prioritize and make the time to communicate all the time — people want to know what is happening where they work.
- Have fun. Both in work and out of work — shared experiences and shared laughter and jokes are the glue that keeps a team together and reminds them of the human interactions and connections that have been formed.

Fig. 8-4 Develop esprit de corps

Key Actions for Clarifying Team Roles and Responsibilities

1. Explain the team's purpose and impact on the organization.
2. Describe the results and standards the team is expected to achieve.
3. Discuss and agree on the roles and responsibilities of each team member.
4. Identify procedures and resources for getting the work done.
5. Encourage team members to figure out and agree on ways to help each other.
6. Summarize and establish a specific follow up plan.

Fig. 8-5 Key Actions for Clarifying Team Roles and Responsibilities

Fig. 8-6 DISC Styles and How They Approach Conflict

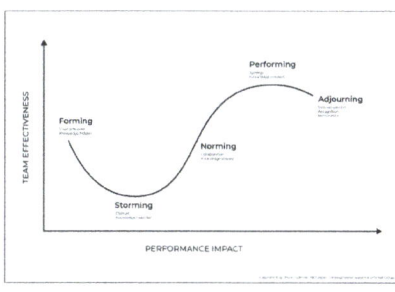

Fig. 8-7 Bruce Tuckman Team Development - with additions

Resources from Chapter 9: **Stay the Course** Follow through with Action Plans

Fig. 9-1 High Performance Checklist

High Performance Checklist

9 SOLUTIONS TO CONQUER THE "MONSTROUS" CHALLENGES IN YOUR BUSINESS

What's the status of yours?

Monster Chapter	Solution Factor	Danger	Caution	Working	Am I Dr. Jekyll	Am I Mr. Hyde	Both at times?
	Shared Mission & Vision	○	○	○	☐	☐	☐
	Organizational Chart Roles & Responsibilities	○	○	○	☐	☐	☐
	Link to Values Beliefs turn into Actions	○	○	○	☐	☐	☐
	Understand & Engage Know Others' Needs	○	○	○	☐	☐	☐
	Top Chaos Creators Processes to Restore Calm	○	○	○	☐	☐	☐
	In Control of Stress & Emotions	○	○	○	☐	☐	☐
	On Top of Cashflow Give to Others	○	○	○	☐	☐	☐
	No More Turmoil Leadership & Culture	○	○	○	☐	☐	☐
	Stay the Course! Use Action Plans	○	○	○	☐	☐	☐
THIS MONTH:	Our Focus is:	○	○	○	☐	☐	☐

LT Brands and Mouth-agape.com

Chapter 10 is **Quick Reference & Resources:**

Forms & Key Actions:

Download files: **www.LTResults.com/monsterbook/resources**

Types of Assessments Mentioned in the Book;
http://LTResults.com/assessments

Email Liz at Liz@LTresults.com for "reader" pricing on assessment links to experience the tools that follow:

> Behavioral Styles (DISC) - How you do what you do
>
> Motivating Drivers - Why you do what you do
>
> Talent Insights Assessment (DISC & Motivating Drivers)
>
> Stress Quotient
>
> Emotional Intelligence Quotient
>
> TriMetrix EQ (DISC, Motivating Drivers & EQ)
>
> And others

* Target Training International Success Insights (TTI) Assessments: *Success Insights® is a registered trademark of Target Training International, Ltd. The Universal Language DISC™ is a trademark of Target Training International, Ltd and its content is a copyright of Target Training International, Ltd. TriMetrix® is a registered trademark of Target Training International Ltd.*

- *Images depicted are property of TTI Success Insights, Used with Permission.*

- *Graphics provided by TTI Success Insights. ©TTI SUCCESS INSIGHTS. ALL RIGHTS RESERVED.*

Recommended Contact for Graphic Work:

Mariia Anikina, Graphic Designer
web: http://anikinadesign.com/
email: marria@anikinadesign.com

The 15 top leadership books every great leader needs on their bookshelf from https://leaders.com

1. The 21 Irrefutable Laws of Leadership

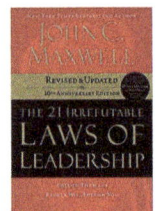

Author: John Maxwell

One-Sentence Description: Maxwell finds the commonalities of great leaders, while also guiding readers through the 21 universal laws of successful leadership.

Favorite Quote: *"I believe the bottom line in leadership isn't how far we advance ourselves but how far we advance others. That is achieved by serving others and adding value to their lives."*

Why You Should Read It: There's a reason it's ranked as one of the best leadership books of all time. Entrepreneurs, executives, and managers find Maxwell's advice useful because it's practical and easy to follow. Furthermore, The 21 Irrefutable Laws of Leadership helps high performers figure out what they've been doing right and play into their strengths. Additionally, the book is beneficial because it offers plenty of ideas on how to fine-tune weaker leadership qualities.

2. Good to Great: Why Some Companies Make the Leap… and Others Don't

Author: Jim Collins

One-Sentence Description: This book follows a five-year study that determines how "good" companies become great, beat their competitors, and achieve long-lasting success.

Favorite Quote: *"Greatness is not a function of circumstance. Greatness, it turns out, is largely a matter of conscious choice, and discipline."*

Why You Should Read It: *Good to Great: Why Some Companies Make the Leap… and Others Don't* emphasizes the point that success doesn't happen overnight.

For entrepreneurs and leaders who feel frustrated, tired, and out of steam, this book helps reinvigorate drive and passion. Additionally, it's comforting to know that many of the difficulties business owners experience as they grow aren't uncommon. In fact, growing pains are evidence that a company is developing. Overall, the core message is progress is a process.

3. Start with Why

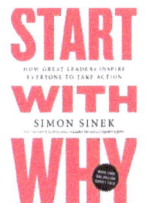

Author: Simon Sinek

One-Sentence Description: Sinek provides a three-step framework that purpose-driven leaders use to inspire people to take action.

Favorite Quote: *"People don't buy what you do; they buy why you do it. And what you do simply proves what you believe."*

Why You Should Read It: *Start with Why* is one of the best leadership books for receiving a foundational understanding of what it means to lead with purpose. Those wanting to refresh and revive their organizations should read this book first. Without a doubt, Start with Why changes the game on how leaders guide their companies. It explains the importance of putting purpose at the center of the business so owners and executives don't lose focus on fulfilling the company's mission. An understanding of how to lead with why has the power to truly transform any business for the better.

4. Think and Grow Rich

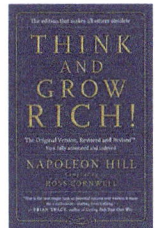

Author: Napoleon Hill

One-Sentence Description: Published in 1937, Think and Grow Rich studies the lives of wealthy individuals such as Henry Ford and Andrew Carnegie, defining 13 habits successful people share.

Favorite Quote: *"The starting point of all achievement is DESIRE. Keep this constantly in mind. Weak desire brings weak results, just as a small fire makes a small amount of heat."*

Why You Should Read It: Consistently ranked as one of the best books on leadership of all time, Think and Grow Rich helps readers understand the unique mindset of high performers. On the whole, Hill spent 25 years researching, analyzing, and understanding what makes people successful. Through 500 interviews, he found and wrote a formula for prosperity. Undoubtedly, the directive strategies are easily applicable, motivational, and provide timeless wisdom to anyone interested in leadership.

5. *Wooden on Leadership*

Author: John Wooden

One-Sentence Description: Famed basketball coach John Wooden explains the 15 principles of success and the characteristics great leaders share.

Favorite Quote: *"The best leaders are lifelong learners; they take measures to create organizations that foster and inspire learning throughout. The most effective leaders are those who realize it's what you learn after you know it all that counts most."*

Why You Should Read It: *Wooden on Leadership* inspires leaders through adages and advice given by one of the most successful coaches in sports history. In summary, Wooden teaches business professionals how to build a great team people love belonging to through his motivational words focused on morals and ethics. Overall, this is a must-read for anyone who wants to build an inspiring, sustainable team culture within their organization.

6. *Extreme Ownership*

Author: Jocko Willink and Leif Babin

One-Sentence Description: Written by two Navy SEAL officers, this best-selling book relates their special operations experience to the leadership qualities all business owners, executives, and managers should possess.

Favorite Quote: *"Implementing Extreme Ownership requires checking your ego and operating with a high degree of humility. Admitting mistakes, taking ownership, and developing a plan to overcome challenges are integral to any successful team."*

Why You Should Read It: The unique, interesting angle the authors take creates a fresh perspective within the genre. While some professionals might not feel this book would be applicable to their businesses, Extreme Ownership teaches lessons that help leaders understand what it truly means to lead—not manage or direct—others. With unique messaging filled with real-life experience, the book additionally provides instruction on how to successfully develop high-performing teams that can fulfill even the most difficult mission.

7. Dare to Lead

Author: Brené Brown

One-Sentence Description: Dare to Lead focuses on building a strong culture at work through vulnerability, courage, core values, and trust.

Favorite Quote: *"I define a leader as anyone who takes responsibility for finding the potential in people and processes, and who has the courage to develop that potential."*

Why You Should Read It: *Dare to Lead* is one of the best leadership books for building team culture. Brown, an accomplished researcher with a Ph.D. in social work, argues the long-standing belief that vulnerability correlates to "weakness" is false. In fact, she writes an entire book to prove that being vulnerable is both courageous and brave. Specifically, this trait is one of the best leadership qualities found in business owners, executives, and managers. For this reason, Dare to Lead is perfect for anyone interested in creating a constructive, supportive workplace. It teaches people how to connect, be more empathetic, and show up with authenticity.

8. The Effective Executive

Author: Peter F. Drucker

One-Sentence Description: This book focuses on effectiveness as a form of self-discipline—a requirement for all leaders (and a skill anyone can learn).

Favorite Quote: *"Intelligence, imagination, and knowledge are essential resources, but only effectiveness converts them into results."*

Why You Should Read It: Success is dependent on effectiveness. From exacting change to inspiring employees, this is a quality leaders can't afford to lack. Nevertheless, many business owners and executives unknowingly or knowingly behave, act, and communicate in ways that don't positively impact their organizations. For example, ineffective leaders lack emotional intelligence and don't dedicate themselves to learning how to become stewards of their employees and customers. In essence, The Effective Executive is for people who want to actively learn how to work on eliminating ineffective leadership traits and become drivers of positive impact.

9. 7 Habits of Highly Effective People

Author: Stephen R. Covey

One-Sentence Description: Covey believes effective people align their values with universal principles—the seven habits describe a person's relation to independence, interdependence, and continuous improvement.

Favorite Quote: *"As you care less about what people think of you, you will care more about what others think of themselves."*

Why You Should Read It: While this leadership book has a simple title, the pages inside reveal Covey's philosophical nature. For instance, Seven Habits of Highly Effective Peopleasks readers to examine themselves by challenging their beliefs, perception, and world view. This book is important for leaders at all levels because it essentially teaches people how to be better, more connected, empathetic humans.

10. The Art of War

Author: Sun Tzu

One-Sentence Description: The Art of War teaches leaders how to create and implement strategic initiatives.

Favorite Quote: *"In the midst of chaos, there is also opportunity."*

Why You Should Read It: Out of all the best leadership books mentioned, this 5th century B.C. military treatise is the oldest. There's a reason it's continued inspiring generations of strategic thinkers. While it was written for military leaders, the text translates well for business owners and executives who are responsible for developing and executing the company's vision. In short, it takes readers through 13 chapters, each dedicated to a particular stage in the strategic implementation process.

11. Awaken the Giant Within

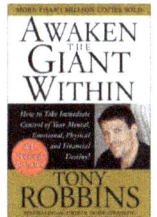

Author: Tony Robbins

One-Sentence Description: World-renowned motivational speaker and coach Tony Robbins helps readers replace their bad habits, retrain their mindset, and increase their happiness so they can step into their greatness.

Favorite Quote: *"Enjoy making decisions. You must know that in any moment a decision you make can change the course of your life forever ... If you really want your life to be passionate, you need to live with this attitude of expectancy."*

Why You Should Read It: Published in 1991, Awaken the Giant Within is full of the passion and charged words people would expect from a young Tony Robbins. As a coach focused on elevating people to their full potential, this is a great read for leaders dissatisfied by mediocracy. Although this book is more targeted toward young entrepreneurs and new business owners, it is a powerful read for those who want to live extraordinary lives as leaders.

12. The 5 Dysfunctions of a Team

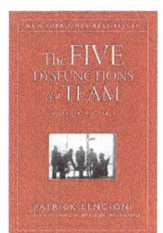

Author: Patrick Lencioni

One-Sentence Description: Lencioni uses his knack for storytelling to resolve five common dysfunctional behaviors that inhibit even the best teams.

Favorite Quote: *"Not finance. Not strategy. Not technology. It is teamwork that remains the ultimate competitive advantage, both because it is so powerful and so rare."*

Why You Should Read It: Leaders must know how to both guide their teams and be a team player. This book stresses the importance of having a cohesive team dynamic. While the book is a fictional fable, it is a story many business owners and executives struggle with. Companies cannot succeed unless their teams work together. For this reason, the book points out dysfunctional behaviors that harm team culture. As a result, leaders can repair and avoid toxicity within their organizations using this insight.

13. *How to Win Friends and Influence People*

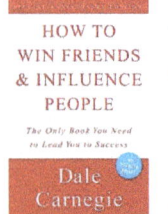

Author: Dale Carnegie

One-Sentence Description: Carnegie's book provides insight on how likability leads to strong relationships, new friends and influence.

Favorite Quote: *"You can't win an argument. You can't because if you lose it, you lose it; and if you win it, you lose it."*

Why You Should Read It: First published in 1936, How to Win Friends and InfluencePeople provides timeless lessons on how to win people over without using manipulation and morally unethical tactics. In essence, this book is a great read that proves likability goes a long way in life. The knowledge provided in Carnegie's work is invaluable to leaders and customer-facing team members, such as sales teams. Additionally, the book teaches you how to advance your interpersonal skills.

14. *Team of Rivals*

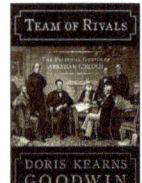

Author: Doris Kearns Goodwin

One-Sentence Description: In this Lincoln biography, Kearns shows how the president united his former political competitors to abolish slavery and win the Civil War.

Favorite Quote: *"In order to 'win a man to your cause,' Lincoln explained, you must first reach his heart, 'the great high road to his reason.'"*

Why You Should Read It: This leadership book is a masterclass on leadership and an interesting read for anyone who loves history. It shows how important it is to toss your ego aside when working with others. Rather than punishing his rivals, Lincoln welcomed several of these people into his cabinet and created a unified front that was capable of holding the country together. While the book has a rather political motif, it teaches executive leaders the value of bringing teams together toward a collective cause. Personal beliefs of individual group members may vary but there can be healthy competition among them, as long as it doesn't get in the way of a larger, common objective.

15. 15 Invaluable Laws of Growth

Author: John C. Maxwell

One-Sentence Description: The third book in Maxwell's "Laws" series provides readers with a new set of principles designed for growth and self-development.

Favorite Quote: *"Most people who decide to grow personally find their first mentors in the pages of books."*

Why You Should Read It: The continuous path of self-improvement differentiates a good leader from a great leader. When starting a business or accepting a leadership role, a person is really accepting the responsibility of dedicating their life to learning how to become better for those they're responsible for guiding. To summarize, Maxwell helps people understand the required growing process and how to apply it to everyday life.

Acknowledgments

When we experience "monstrous" problems in our business (and lives) we normally feel alone and isolated. We believe no one else understands or can help us. That statement applied to me when I first thought about writing a book, but the evolution of *Who's Leading Your Business?* has proved otherwise.

Through the years I'd heard people say, "You should write a book." As much as I wanted to do just that I'd sarcastically reply, "Right. I wouldn't even know where to start, it's too overwhelming." I knew I was a strong speaker, but an author? I wasn't sure I was qualified.

My friends, Ann Holland, Ph.D., J.J. Lesley, Ph.D., Erin Hutton, Ph.D., Heidi Blossom, Ph.D., had told me their tales of the time, energy, and research that had gone into writing their thesis'. It sounded horrifying! Then last year Ann Holland, Ph.D., published, *Self-Motivation Mastery* during the pandemic. I was totally in awe! I really wanted to author a book, but because all my writer friends were Ph.D.'s, I was sure I needed one too before I could begin.

Then my dear friend, Anna Lam-Decker in the U.K,. asked me to check out the Self-Publishing School based in my home state of South Carolina. She wanted to have them coach her through writing a book and to ensure they were not a scam. Be it coincidence or divine intervention, I checked them out and was so impressed that I immediately signed up as a student and an advocate. That "coincidence" was my first reminder that the universe provides help in some form when we need it—if we ask.

The team at the Self-Publishing School matched me perfectly to my coach, Scott Allan. Scott's background as a successful author gave me the confidence to begin my own author journey. His knowledge and guidance got me to the finish line.

At this point I was still just starting. I had overcome my block to the idea of writing a book, but soon another "monstrous problem" presented itself. My initial book outline crossed intellectual property lines and couldn't be written. I was crushed, lost, and still financially committed to writing some kind of book.

In the middle of this book-writing crisis, another dear friend, Padraig Hyland, CEO of The Core Story, reached out from Ireland. A divine intervention? He, Anna and I had worked together in Hong Kong. Padraig encouraged me to keep on, brainstormed ideas with me, and let me know that I had the stories to make a book work.

As I developed my new concept, I wondered if there was a way to integrate my son Cole's illustrations into the book and create a joint project. I sensed that the wry wit of his art would add a memorable dimension to my content. When we talked, his creative mind took off. In less than five minutes he had brainstormed numerous potential book titles that he believed could combine our work successfully.

As I quickly considered the feasibility of the concept, I recalled Cole's visit to meet my client /friend, Jennifer Paradis, CEO of The Signatures Company. Jen had shown Cole ideas for how to use his art in various business applications –that helped me realize this collaboration would work! My excitement sparked to know we could do this together.

But my inspiration only lasted until the next "monstrous problem" awoke. After I'd written the rough draft I took off to Iowa for a short vacation to see my siblings and share my book news. During that time, I realized that the real work was just beginning. I had to self-edit the entire book–which would be like rewriting it **again**. I felt overwhelmed as I realized I also needed professional editors.

During the visit, my sister Susan Retz, an artist and owner of Comfort and Ease Ortho-Bionomy™ and Holistic Centering, told me she'd considered being an editor, who knew? I asked her to be my content editor. She successfully married Cole's illustrative monster images and my business concepts into this entertaining and informative resource with quippy verbiage. Thank you Sue! Coincidence or divine intervention?

On my return home, I had lunch with my girlfriend, Johanna Inman, President of Ideal HR, who I knew had an art degree. I lamented my need for a professional line editor. Johanna offered to introduce me to her sister, Sara Jurand, as a potential editorial solution, then offered herself, and her mother, Melinda Hoffman, who is also an artist, to provide me whatever expertise I needed throughout the book-writing process. Suddenly, a whole team of support people materialized in one lunch! A coincidence? I think not. It started because I asked…then received.

Sara Jurand, thank you for responding to my need for an editor. I appreciate the time, professionalism and dedication you showed to this process. Your gifts are not mine! As Sara asked about formatting the book, I realized I had to have more professional looking forms and resources to share with my readers. The quest turned to find a forms person.

Mariia Anikina, with Upwork, fit the bill. Thank you for your diligent work, reading my mind when my instructions were unclear, and creating my forms and graphs throughout the book.

Heidi Blossom, Ph.D., coincidentally stepped in at that point to use her expertise as my digital marketing department. She upgraded my branding, built a new website, and provided additional media and audio recording expertise to ensure that my book launch aligned with my strategic consulting business. I am so grateful for her time and support as I wrote this book. Erin's too!

The support continued with the Steelworks leadership team – Thank you – J.J., Paul, Rick, Brad, and Mr. Jimmy for regularly feeding me lunch as I tried out phrases and images to see how they'd land with my potential readers. JJ, thanks for your guidance and keeping me on track.

Lastly, my biggest thank you to my husband Dan who allowed me to share his stories, read rough drafts, and offered his brother, Mick Parker's expertise. Dan cooked meals or ate alone while I wrote, edited and stressed. He kept my coffee full at 5:30 a.m. and held his tongue when I landed in bed at 2 a.m. Thank you, my love, for your support and the confidence that I could do this.

And so, we are never alone in anything we do. The web of people and circumstances behind the writing of this book is my proof. I have not highlighted all who supported me, but please know, I am grateful to all my clients, friends, and family for their words of encouragement. Thanks to each of you and thanks to our Creator who unites us all!

Author Bio - Liz Parker

Liz's business quest started when she founded LT Consultants Inc. in 1999 in Hong Kong as a strategic planning consultant, team alignment facilitator and executive performance coach, who is now based in Greer, SC. She is also a Vistage speaker and YPO guest speaker.

Liz coaches leaders at all levels and across all industries to greater self-awareness and the hidden potential in themselves and their businesses. She engaged her son, Cole, to join her on this book-writing quest with the purpose of co-creating a memorable context for strategic thinking and leadership development. In the process they had some "monstrous" fun together!

Liz's certifications include:

Behavioral, Motivators, and HD Analyst through TTI Success Insights. https://www.ttisi.com

Growth Curve Strategist for the 7 Stages of Entrepreneurial growth through Flashpoint! https://www.igniteyourbiz.com

GROW® Coach through BMW - https://www.insideoutdev.com

Rhythm Maker in Razor Coach program for Catipult.ai, strategic implementation software, https://www.catipult.ai

She has worked with multi-national organizations in worldwide leadership development, cross-functional team dynamics, strategic planning and coaching across Asia-Pacific, Australia, Europe and the UK, the Middle East, South America, and the U.S.

Liz loves traveling with her husband Dan. They enjoy visiting their three children's families to see grandkids and grandpets. She loves deep conversation over good food and playing noncompetitive golf in 60+°F!

Website: www.LTResults.com; Email: Liz@LTresults.com; Phone: 1.864.382.0304

Next Steps/How to Work with Me

You may be wondering - **What's Next?**

If you haven't already received my free gift, the High-Performance Checklist go to: www.LTResults.com/monsterbook/resources to download your free copy now.

I encourage you to download the poster version to print and hang on your office wall, maybe even laminate it, to reuse each month. Hold a monthly meeting with your leaders to focus on the topic most pressing. Address each of the problems and evaluate how you each lead, that is to say, are you Jekyll or Hyde-like?

When you download the checklist, please, "opt in" to stay connected with me and you'll receive my monthly video blogs to remind you of important points or new information that you and your leadership team can reference throughout the month.

If you would like to explore how to work with me, access assessments or surveys, create higher performing teams and leaders, email me at Liz@LTResults.com, call 1.864.382.0304, or visit www.LTResults.com. Let's explore your needs!

CAN YOU HELP?

Love this book? Don't forget to leave a review!

Every review matters, and it matters a *lot!*

Head over to Amazon or wherever you purchased this book to leave an honest review for me.

I sincerely appreciate the time you spent reading /listening and thank you!

Liz Parker

selfpublishing.com

NOW IT'S YOUR TURN

**Discover the EXACT 3-step blueprint you need to become
a bestselling author in as little as 3 months.**

Self-Publishing School helped me, and now I want them to help

you with this FREE resource to begin outlining your book!

Even if you're busy, bad at writing, or don't know where to start,

you CAN write a bestseller and build your best life.

With tools and experience across a variety of niches and

professions,

Self-Publishing School is the <u>only</u> resource you need to

take your book to the finish line!

DON'T WAIT

Say "YES" to becoming a bestseller:

https://selfpublishing.com/friend/

Follow the steps on the page to get a FREE resource to get
started on your book and unlock a discount to get started with
SelfPublishing.com

Want our help implementing the content in this book?

At Self Publishing School, our goal is to save you 100's of hours and $1,000's of dollars in the process...and to help you write a better book that sells more copies.

If you want to go faster further with your book and you're serious about getting our help, book a call with the team to put together a plan and see how we can help:

PUBLISHEDBOOK.COM/APPLY